AF492281

UNMASKING

A JOURNEY THROUGH TRAUMA, TRUTH, AND A SPECTRUM OF HEALING

KAITLYN KENEALY MA, LPC

Kaitlyn Elizabeth Kenealy, MA, LPC
Unmasking: A Journey Through Trauma, Truth, and a Spectrum of Healing

Wildroot Press
Copyright © 2026 by Kaitlyn Elizabeth Kenealy, MA, LPC

First Edition
Hardcover ISBN 979-8-9998719-0-9
Softcover ISBN 979-8-9998719-1-6
eBook ISBN 979-8-9998719-2-3
Audiobook ISBN 979-8-9998719-3-0

All rights reserved under International and Pan-American Copyright Conventions. Manufactured in the United States of America.

No part of this publication may be reproduced, stored in, or introduced into a retrieval system, transmitted in any form or by any means (electronic, mechanical, photocopying, recording, or otherwise), and/or otherwise used in any manner for purposes of training artificial intelligence technologies to generate text, including, without limitation, technologies that are capable of generating works in the same style or genre as this publication, without the prior written permission of the publisher.

This book is sold subject to the condition that it shall not, by way of trade or otherwise, be lent, resold, hired out, or otherwise circulated without the publisher's prior written consent in any form of binding, cover, or condition other than that in which it was published.

Book Design | Alicia Kowalewski
Editor | Kathie Lynas
Author Portrait Photography | Kim Kedinger Photography
Publishing Management | TSPA The Self Publishing Agency, Inc.

Dedication

For anyone who has ever been asked to dim their light, silence their truth, or shrink themselves to fit a version of the world that was never made for them—This book is for you.

May you unmask unapologetically.

May you take up space without shame.

May you come home to the truth of who you are.

To my patients—past, present, and future—Thank you for allowing me into your stories. Your vulnerability, courage, and willingness to face the hard things have shaped me more than words can express. You've challenged me to show up with integrity, to do my own inner work, and to live the healing I speak about.

This book would not exist without you.

You are the reason I believe healing is possible.

You are the reason I kept going.

And to my brother—Your absence cracked me open, but your love continues to guide me.

I made a promise that I would write your name in the sky.

This book is part of that promise. You are in every page, every word, every light I turn back on.

A Message to My Readers: The Second Time Around

Here I am again offering my story, my scars, and my truth in the hope that it helps you feel less alone.

This book isn't just a continuation of my journey; it's a deeper reckoning.

If *Healing is Messy AF* was a controlled burn—raw, emotional, but contained—this book is the aftermath. The slow excavation of what remained buried beneath the ash. It's not just about unmasking. It's about asking why we ever needed the mask in the first place.

Writing this has been less of a process and more of a purge. Every chapter required me to hold eye contact with truths I had long avoided—to feel them fully, name them clearly, and let them move through me in ways they hadn't before. This time, the wounds didn't just ache—they demanded attention.

This book was never about being polished.

It was about being real.

Real in the discomfort.

Real in the questions.

Real in the mess.

Because healing, as I've learned again and again, is anything but linear. It loops. It lingers. It returns in waves. And it doesn't happen in isolation.

This is a companion for those of you walking through your own spectrum of healing—for those ready not just to take off the mask, but to examine what's underneath. To confront the silence, the expectations, the patterns, and the pain. To ask the deeper questions. To return to yourself.

If you're here, reading this, you're already doing the work. Already healing—whether it feels like progress or not.

So, wherever you are in your process:

Keep going.

You don't have to do it perfectly.

You just have to keep showing up.

I'll be right here beside you.

—Kaitlyn

Contents

Introduction

The Girl in the Yellow Dress: Confronting the Shadows and Unraveling the Mask

I don't know exactly when she first appeared—only that she's always been there.

Sometimes she's in the corner of a memory, sunlit and soft, with something bold in her eyes. Sometimes she walks ahead of me in dreams, barefoot in grass, the hem of her yellow dress catching wind like a flag daring me to follow. Other times, she's quiet in the corner of my mind, waiting for me to notice her. Waiting to be named.

Who is the girl in the yellow dress?

Is she me before the world asked me to be smaller, quieter, easier to digest?

Is she the version I buried under perfectionism, professionalism, and people-pleasing?

Is she the truth I tucked away beneath trauma?

Yellow, to me, has always meant something—warmth, vitality, defiance. But it's also the color of caution. A flare against fog. The edge before the unraveling. This girl in the yellow dress isn't always smiling. She's not here to be palatable. She's here to be seen—fully—and maybe even to see me back. I've come to believe she is all of me. The before, the after, the in-between. A reminder of what I was forced to let go of. And who I am now choosing to reclaim.

This book is about her.

About me.

About all of us who've been hiding in plain sight.

I began writing this book as a deeper exploration of trauma. But what unfolded was something far more expansive. As I peeled back the layers of my story, I began uncovering pieces of myself I didn't know I had buried. In the process of healing trauma, I discovered I am neurodivergent—something I had never considered until I began unmasking.

This realization was not a detour from the trauma work—it was a direct result of it.

We often speak of "unmasking" in relation to autism, but the metaphor goes deeper. We all wear masks to survive. My mask was built out of trauma, reinforced by systems that demanded I perform, excel, and please. That mask made me successful, but it also made me exhausted. Stripped of that mask, I didn't just discover autism—I discovered authenticity.

Unraveling the Early Layers

Trauma doesn't always arrive as one devastating moment. Sometimes, it's cumulative—a series of unmet needs, subtle betrayals, and moments of silence that slowly chip away at your sense of safety. Looking back, I can see how trauma threaded itself through my early life.

I was raised by a single mother of four. We had no car, no internet, no hot water unless we boiled it on the stove. And while my mother's love was steady, so was the instability. My father—mostly absent—started a new family where things appeared more "normal." I lived between these two worlds: the youngest in one house and the oldest in the other, constantly adapting, always aware of how little control I had.

In elementary school, I was involved in everything—sports, student council, school plays. I was the golden child on the outside. But inside, I was starting to fracture. The first "C" I ever received in school felt like a failure so deep it shook my self-concept. I began measuring my worth through performance—and I never stopped.

Adolescence and the Loss of Safety

Middle school brought the first major rupture. At a time when I was already trying to adapt to a new social world, I experienced a traumatic sexual assault that left lasting scars. What followed was months of stalking and harassment by the perpetrator—both inside and outside of school. It destroyed any sense of safety I had left.

But I told no one. I carried that secret. I let it devour me.

And in the silence, I turned to coping strategies that felt like survival: oversexualization, defiance, drinking, and using. I moved in with my father, hoping to outrun the pain—only to realize I had brought it with me. I returned home a year later, broken, numb, and still silent.

I barely graduated high school. I missed walking across the stage. My mother, heartbroken but cautious, did her best to support me without pushing me away. I still ache when I think of how I hurt her by leaving. But I also understand now—I was running from shame I didn't have the language to name.

The Long Road to Healing

The spiral continued until I hit the point where survival felt optional. There were mornings I begged God to take me instead of my younger brother. I cried until I couldn't breathe—and then I went to work anyway. After his suicide, that pain only deepened. The guilt, the grief, the unbearable weight of knowing we shared similar wounds… but only one of us made it out alive.

And yet—I stayed. I stayed in the field. I kept showing up for others. Because through it all, I knew what it was like to feel invisible. I knew what it was like to carry a secret. I knew what it meant to be trapped in your own body, smiling on the outside while screaming inside. That's why I'm a therapist. That's why I wrote this book.

Confronting the Shadows

So many of us say "my childhood was good" when what we mean is "I survived it." We minimize. We deny. We resist the term "trauma" because we know what it means: if there was harm, there is accountability. And accountability—especially when it threatens to rewrite the stories we were told by the people we love—is terrifying.

But the truth is this: Trauma thrives in silence. Healing requires confrontation—not with rage, but with radical honesty.

When I began this journey, I thought I was writing about

trauma. Then I realized I was writing about self-abandonment. Then neurodivergence. Then authenticity. In the end, I was writing about all of it—because healing doesn't happen in separate compartments. It's layered. It's cyclical. And it demands that we see the full picture, not just the polished version.

This is not a story of blame. It is a story of becoming.

Of taking off the mask.

Of seeing the girl in the yellow dress—the one who always knew who she was—and daring to meet her in the light.

And if you've been hiding behind your own mask, I hope you see yourself here too.

Let's begin.

Part One

THE MASK
& THE WOUND

Chapter 1
THE ARCHITECTURE OF THE MASK

I didn't build the mask all at once.

It was crafted slowly—forged in silence, shame, and the quiet desperation to be accepted.

I learned early on that being *me* wasn't safe. That my reactions were "too much," my emotions inconvenient, my instincts too intense. So, I started to observe. To study. To shape-shift. I watched how other people moved through the world—what made them fit in, what made them safe, what made them liked. I became a master mimic without even realizing it. My mom would always call me a "chameleon." I could fit in everywhere and with everyone.

I don't know how old I was when I first began doing it, but I do remember the feeling. The sense that if I could just get it *right*, if I could act the right way, say the right thing, wear the right smile, then I'd belong. Then maybe no one would see the parts of me I feared were too strange, too broken, too "other."

So, I adapted.

I built the mask out of likability.

Out of good grades. Out of people-pleasing. Out of charm, accomplishment, and a high tolerance for emotional discomfort. I learned to read a room before I ever walked into it.

I learned how to mirror people so they felt comfortable—even if I didn't.

I learned to silence my instincts if they made other people uncomfortable.

And I learned to dissociate so smoothly I could sit in a room full of people and feel absolutely invisible—and still call that a win.

Because at least they weren't rejecting me.

They weren't seeing *her*—the real me. The unfiltered, intuitive, tender, messy version that had never quite seemed welcome.

The mask became my safety.

It got me through school.

It got me into rooms I never thought I'd be allowed in.

It helped me become "successful," even as I was quietly unraveling.

But it came at a cost.

When you spend so much time becoming who others need you to be, you forget who *you* are. You lose the sound of your own voice beneath the noise of performance. You stop trusting your gut—and start confusing survival with identity.

And the hardest part?

The mask worked.

It worked so well that even *I* forgot I was wearing it. It's through the grief of losing my brother that it has officially fallen off, which meant I had to find her, the real me, again.

Steeling Yourself for the Trauma Journey

Layered in Yellow

In the corridors of memory, a vision unfolds,
A girl in a yellow dress, her story retold.
A younger self, bathed in innocence's light,
Trusting, carefree, a spirit shining bright.
In the kaleidoscope of joy, she once danced,
Loving all, a heart completely entranced.
Oh, how I yearn for that radiant past,
The echo of laughter, too beautiful to last.
The yellow dress, a symbol of days so divine,
I wish its embrace could once again be mine.
In the echoes of time, where nostalgia rests,
Yearning for the girl in the yellow dress.

From a clinician's perspective, I specialize in trauma and can effectively walk with patients down that path. Not only can I relate on a professional level but also on a personal level. Of course, it's imperative that I don't make sessions about myself, but if the time is appropriate and if something resonates, I try to make a connection with my own story.

It's a delicate balance—a type of dance—between the art and science of what we do as clinicians. I was drawn to becoming a therapist because I was always interested in getting to the root of an issue, and I also wanted to offer people a different path from the one I traveled. I knew many of the things I personally experienced or witnessed were not "regular." (I try to not say "normal" because that doesn't exist.)

People's trauma varies, and most people walk through my office door and state that their childhood was "normal." I validate their perceptions and smile in my mind, as I know that we will be making connections at some point on how their childhood played a role in their adult life, positive and negative.

People often have negative feelings when exploring childhood for a plethora of reasons, such as guilt, shame, and holding family secrets. Often, they want to reassure me that "it wasn't that bad," and their parents aren't bad people. I acknowledge the truth of those statements, while adding that we need to explore those earlier years to understand what is affecting us today.

Patients also stress they don't want to "blame," and I often redirect and reframe our work together as an exploration, not a blame game. "Let's uncover all the puzzle pieces and process them," I explain.

If I am asking others to explore and uncover, it only feels fair that I do so myself. Although writing this book has made me feel like I am digging up and regurgitating the trauma that I felt I had healed over and over. Clearly, there is nothing easy about coming to therapy, being a therapist, or even writing about your trauma. In fact, most people bury, deny, and avoid, which in the moment feels better, but unresolved trauma often comes out in symptoms, such as anxiety, depression, PTSD, health issues, and many more.

So again, I always try to emphasize that we are treating the symptoms, and these symptoms are not your identity. You are not anxiety and you are not depression. They are symptoms to be treated and to do so, we need to know where, when, and how they came about, which is often childhood. See how that puzzle fits!

I like to be about work and do the inner work that helps me heal myself along with my patients.

I was recently doing some inner child work, which I highly recommend for anyone doing trauma work. Louise Hay, my inspiration for connecting with my inner child, has been pivotal in my "me-search"—a term I learned from some amazing women that have a podcast that I was featured on, called *Red Couch Rebels*. (I am proud to use the term, but it's imperative that I give a huge shout-out to these two amazing humans who are also about the work!)

Back to my "me-search." I'd like to take you back to one moment I experienced in that journey.

I have just closed the workbook about inner child work and am deep in my "feels" and contemplating my healing. I start thinking back to my innocence and ask myself if I can remember the last time I felt pure, unashamed of myself, and joyful/playful. Then I see myself in the yellow dress that features in the poem earlier in this chapter. I vividly see myself laughing, dancing, running around, and just full of life. I remember her. I start to feel her.

Part of the inner work is asking or remembering what that inner child needs to feel safe. (By the way, we have many inner versions of ourselves. The teenage one is probably the one I fear and love the most.) I am thinking about her (which is me) and start to miss those feelings and that unfiltered little girl who loved life and who had no reason yet not to trust. I think about how I longed to get back to her and what she needs, but this isn't the time.

I recognize I have a session soon, so I need to shelve these thoughts and emotions for the moment. I remember taking a deep breath, and then my phone lit up. I grabbed it off my desk and saw it was a message from Kimmy, my mom.

She said, "I was going through old pictures and look what I found." She had sent a picture of me in that yellow dress! My mouth dropped open and my eyes widened. The emotions flooded back, and I remembered everything that version of me had felt all those years ago. Now, as I sat back in my chair, I felt like the girl in the yellow dress sat on my lap and comforted me, telling me that I was going to be okay.

I truly believe there are no coincidences in the world. In that moment, God, the universe/or whatever force you believe in was sending me a sign that I was on the right path to continue doing the inner work. (And I have.)

Whether you ask for signs or they show up unbidden, you need to be in a healing or open state to receive them and interpret and understand them. That's what healing is; it is not linear and it's not always clear, but you must be reconnected to your nervous system in order to truly process. You cannot continue down the path of burying, denying, and avoiding.

I definitely understand this denial pattern and can relate! But once you do decide to do the work the trauma only comes back amplified, as the only way to heal is to feel. Let me say that again, the only way to heal is to feel!

Now is your journey going to look like mine? Absolutely not! It's not supposed to, as each person's journey is unique. You need to do your own inner work, but you can learn from my story, and I can learn from yours. It's the interconnectedness that creates a ripple effect, and the more we heal ourselves on our own and together, the more we can change the world. John Lennon is singing in my head right now—"Imagine"—but truthfully, it starts with us as individuals and then community and connecting. I work with a diverse range of individuals, but the stories all weave together and are similar in many aspects.

Chapter 2

THE FIRST CRACK

Grief has a way of breaking what you didn't know was already fragile.

When I lost my brother, everything cracked open—including the mask.

Until then, I had mastered the art of appearing composed. I had performed my life with precision: high-achieving, reliable, polished. The kind of woman who could carry everyone else's pain, hold space, get the job done, and still smile in photos. I knew how to stay busy. How to bury myself in degrees, in ambition, in fixing other people. That drive was praised—admired even. But it wasn't *just* drive. It was trauma drive.

It looked like ambition on the outside.

But on the inside, it was survival.

Trauma drive pushes you to succeed not for joy—but for safety. To keep moving, to keep achieving, to never sit still long enough for the past to catch up to you. It did help me build a life. It helped me stay functional. It even saved me in a thousand little ways. But here's the truth no one talks about: Trauma drive is productive, but it is not sustainable.

It burns hot and fast.

And eventually, it burns you out.

When my brother died, there was no amount of productivity that could shield me from it. There was no degree, no next big thing, no project to pour myself into that could absorb that kind of pain. The mask didn't protect me then—it *shattered*.

Grief didn't care how well I could perform stability.

It brought me to my knees, and suddenly the version of myself I had spent decades curating didn't make sense anymore. She couldn't hold what I was feeling. She wasn't built for *this*. And maybe . . . she never really was.

That loss exposed everything—not just my heart, but my patterns.

The way I used busyness as a numbing agent.

The way I chased validation like it was oxygen.

The way I stayed in relationships long after they stopped feeling like home because I thought being chosen was the same thing as being loved.

It was the beginning of a different kind of awareness.

Not instant. Not neat. But undeniable.

I started to see the rollercoaster for what it was—not a thrill ride, but a trauma loop. Highs that looked like success followed by crashes of disconnection and burnout. The mask wasn't just heavy now—it was splintered. And through those cracks, I caught glimpses of someone I barely recognized.

Maybe . . . the real me.

The Many Faces of Trauma (Because It's Never Just One Thing)

Trauma is not a one-size-fits-all experience.

It's not just "big" events or headline moments.

It's the quiet ruptures, the lingering shame, the patterns that live in our bones and ripple through generations.

It affects individuals, families, and entire communities. It can be loud, violent, and obvious—or silent, invisible, and just as damaging.

Understanding the different types of trauma is like finally having a map for the territory you've always been walking through blind.

And for me, once I started learning about trauma clinically, it was like someone handed me the cheat codes to my own life.

Addiction in the family? Yep.

Generational anxiety and depression? Check.

A cycle of emotional suppression and caretaking? Absolutely.

And here's the thing: Knowing where it came from doesn't excuse my behavior—but it *does* give me the power to change it.

To stop the script. To write a new one. To regulate my nervous system.

1. Developmental Trauma
The Foundation of the Self

This is the trauma that starts young—before we have words.

It happens when our basic emotional needs aren't met in childhood, and our nervous system adapts to survive in an unpredictable or unsafe environment.

Examples: Emotional neglect, inconsistent parenting, abuse, witnessing domestic violence.
Impact: Low self-worth, difficulty trusting others, chronic anxiety, emotional dysregulation.

The way we were loved as children becomes the voice we hear inside our heads as adults.

2. Historical Trauma
The Pain Passed Through Generations

This trauma doesn't start with us—but it lives in us.
It's inherited. Carried through lineage. Repeated in systems.

Examples: Colonization, genocide, slavery, forced assimilation, systemic racism.
Impact: Collective grief, cultural loss, identity struggles, intergenerational PTSD.

Trauma doesn't disappear—it's carried in DNA, behaviors, and belief systems . . . until we choose to heal it.

3. Chronic Trauma
A Long-Term Warzone

When trauma becomes a constant—not just one event, but a way of life. You live in survival mode for so long that peace feels suspicious.

Examples: Domestic violence, long-term bullying, financial instability, growing up with an unpredictable caregiver.

Impact: Hypervigilance, dissociation, chronic illness, difficulty relaxing or trusting.

If chaos was your comfort zone, healing might feel boring at first. Stick with it anyway.

4. Acute Trauma
The One-Shot Shock to the System

This is the trauma people recognize: the "big event." A single moment that shatters your sense of safety.

Examples: Car accidents, sexual assault, natural disasters, sudden death.
Impact: PTSD, panic attacks, hyperarousal, fear of being "out of control."

Even one moment can rewire your nervous system. But you can learn to rewire it back.

5. Vicarious & Secondary Trauma
The Pain We Absorb from Helping Others

As a therapist, I live here.
This is the cost of caring deeply. Of sitting with other people's pain for a living (or as a parent, caregiver, or empath).

Examples: Therapists, healthcare workers, teachers, first responders, those witnessing trauma.
Impact: Emotional fatigue, burnout, irritability, cynicism, compassion collapse.

You can't heal others by bleeding yourself dry.

6. Repetitive Trauma
The Slow Burn

It's not just the big stuff.
It's the little betrayals. The daily dismissals. The pain that compounds over time.

Examples: Repeated breakups, constant job insecurity, chronic medical trauma, ongoing microaggressions.
Impact: Anxiety, mistrust, feeling unsafe in "normal" environments.

It's death by a thousand emotional papercuts.

7. Complex Trauma (C-PTSD)
When Trauma Becomes a Personality Trait

This is what happens when multiple, long-term traumas become your operating system. Especially in childhood, when the brain is still wiring itself.

Examples: Repeated abuse, neglect, captivity, long-term toxic relationships.
Impact: Identity confusion, people-pleasing, shame spirals, emotional dysregulation.

You're not "too much." You just had to survive a world that gave you too little.

8. Repressed Trauma
The Trauma That Hides . . . Until It Doesn't

Sometimes your brain tucks trauma away to protect you—until it resurfaces like a tidal wave.

Examples: Forgotten childhood abuse, trauma unearthed during therapy, eye movement desensitization and reprocessing (EMDR), or bodywork.
Impact: Flashbacks, emotional flooding, chronic anxiety, physical symptoms.

Your mind may forget. Your body never does.

9. Psychological Trauma
The Mind's Invisible Bruises

Just because it wasn't physical doesn't mean it didn't hurt. Emotional abuse wounds just as deeply—and sometimes more silently.

Examples: Gaslighting, public humiliation, emotional manipulation.
Impact: Self-doubt, low self-esteem, anxiety, identity distortion.

Gaslighting is trauma in slow motion.

10. Physical Trauma
The Body Keeps the Score

When your body is harmed, your psyche doesn't just walk away untouched.

Examples: Physical assault, major surgeries, severe illness.
Impact: PTSD, body shame, mistrust in bodily signals, hyperarousal.

Healing trauma means listening to your body—not overriding it.

11. Sexual Trauma
When Your Body Doesn't Feel Like Home Anymore

This is a trauma that creates deep fractures in identity, safety, and self-worth.
Examples: Rape, molestation, harassment, coercion.
Impact: PTSD, shame, intimacy challenges, disconnection from body.

It was never your fault. It will never be your fault.

12. Collective Trauma
When the Whole World Hurts

Mass events that shake entire communities and leave a collective scar.

Examples: Pandemics, war, genocide, school shootings, 9/11.
Impact: Widespread grief, hypervigilance, social distrust, numbing.

Trauma is not just personal. It's cultural. It's generational. It's systemic.

The Body Remembers, Even If You Don't

Repressed trauma is like an attic box gathering dust—until something triggers it open.

It might show up as gut issues. Autoimmune flares. Panic attacks that "come out of nowhere."

You're not broken.

You're responding exactly how your body was trained to.

Healing is not about "getting over it."

It's about getting through it—*with* your body, not against it.

Breaking the Cycle: Healing Through Awareness

Understanding trauma types helped me realize:

- I wasn't weak.
- I wasn't alone.
- I was adapting to survive.

And now that I know better, I get to choose differently.
So do you.
This chapter isn't here to diagnose you.
It's here to give you language—so you can start naming what hurt you, what shaped you, and what you're ready to outgrow.
You don't need to be everything to everyone anymore.
You don't need to carry it all alone.
You just need to begin.

Trauma Responses—Fight, Flight, Freeze, Fawn & Flop

Trauma responses—fight, flight, freeze, fawn, and flop—aren't just emotional reactions. They are deeply embedded survival mechanisms, written into our nervous systems to protect us from harm. The brain doesn't know the difference between a tiger chasing us or a partner gaslighting us. Danger is danger, and our bodies respond accordingly.

Learning about these responses changed my life. For the first time, I could see myself clearly—not as someone who was broken or "too much," but as someone who was adapting. I wasn't a failure for shutting down or running away. I wasn't weak for people-pleasing or collapsing under pressure. I was surviving. My nervous system had created a blueprint for safety, and I had followed it—often without realizing it.

This is why knowing your trauma response matters.

When we understand the *how* and *why* behind our reactions, we gain the power to pause, to reflect, and to choose differently. We stop blaming ourselves and start supporting ourselves.

Your trauma response isn't your personality. It's your nervous system's best attempt at protection.

And the goal of healing isn't to erase these patterns—it's to meet them with awareness and build the internal safety to respond rather than react.

Let's break down the five major trauma responses and how they might show up in your life.

1. Fight: The Warrior Response

When survival means standing your ground.

Description: You confront threats head-on. Your nervous system prepares for battle—whether physical, emotional, or verbal.

Physical Signs: Increased heart rate, clenched fists, jaw tightness, heat in the chest, adrenaline surge.

Behavioral Signs: Aggression, defiance, argumentativeness, control-seeking, self-sabotage.

Personal Reflection: *For years, I thought anger was dangerous. I feared what would happen if I let it out. But now, I understand that anger is a boundary—it shows us where we've been hurt. The work isn't to silence it. It's to let it speak without letting it destroy.*

2. Flight: The Escape Route

When survival means leaving—physically, mentally, or emotionally.

Description: You feel an overwhelming urge to escape, avoid, or distract yourself from distress.

Physical Signs: Restlessness, pacing, hyperactivity, difficulty focusing, anxiety.

Behavioral Signs: Avoidance, perfectionism, workaholism, impulsively quitting jobs or relationships.

Personal Reflection: *I know I'm in flight mode when everything feels too loud and I want to run. My nervous system hits "evacuate" mode. I used to think this made me flaky or unreliable. Now I know: It was just the only way I knew how to feel safe.*

3. Freeze: The Shutdown

When survival means disappearing.

Description: Your body and mind go still. Everything slows or stops.

Physical Signs: Numbness, blank stare, brain fog, disconnection.

Behavioral Signs: Procrastination, zoning out, dissociation, analysis paralysis.

Personal Reflection: *Freeze was my default for a long time. It let me stay in rooms I didn't want to be in without having to fight or flee. But long-term, it robbed me of my agency. Learning how to gently reawaken from freeze—without forcing myself—has been one of my greatest lessons.*

4. Fawn: The People-Pleasing Trap

When survival means being likable at all costs.

Description: You shape-shift to avoid conflict or rejection.

Physical Signs: Nervous energy, smiling through discomfort, tight throat.

Behavioral Signs: Over-apologizing, saying "yes" when you mean "no," prioritizing others.

Personal Reflection: *Fawning was my masterpiece. I built an entire mask out of likability. It made me successful, accepted . . . and exhausted. I used to think people-pleasing was kindness. But true kindness includes yourself.*

5. Flop: The Collapse

When survival means complete surrender.

Description: Your body shuts down to conserve energy. It's the trauma equivalent of pulling the plug.

Physical Signs: Lethargy, heaviness, blankness, feeling limp.

Behavioral Signs: Hopelessness, resignation, checked out, emotionally numb.

Personal Reflection: *I didn't know what flop was until my body started doing it for me. One minute I'd be trying to hold it all together … the next, I couldn't move. It wasn't laziness. It was shutdown. Learning the difference between rest and collapse changed everything.*

The Trauma Response Spiral

Here's the thing no one tells you: Most of us don't have just *one* trauma response.

We fawn until we fight.
We run until we freeze.
We freeze until we collapse.
It's not linear. It's a spiral. And once you start paying attention

to your patterns, you'll begin to see how survival instincts shaped so much of your life—and how healing asks you to build a new way forward.

Trauma wired your brain for survival. Healing rewires it for safety. You don't have to stay trapped in the same loop. You can learn to respond from your wise mind, not your wounded one.

Chapter 3

WHEN HELPING ISN'T ENOUGH

Out of all the trauma I've carried—and there's been more than I wish there was—losing my brother is the one that broke through my core. It didn't just crack the mask. It obliterated it.

Because how do you stay a healer when one of the people you love the most was in pain you couldn't reach?

How do you sit with clients and believe in the power of therapy when the one person you would've given anything to save is *gone*?

I have built my life, my degrees, my career, my identity around helping others. And when he died, a question looped in my head that I still haven't silenced:

What good am I as a clinician if I couldn't help my own brother?

That thought has haunted me more than anything else.

I know—logically—that it's not that simple.

Grief never is.

Suicide never is.

But logic doesn't always get the final word when trauma is speaking.

I've sat with clients since then—countless clients—holding space, offering tools, bearing witness to their pain. And I've kept going not because I have it all figured out, but because in some strange, aching way, every person I help brings me closer to him.

Maybe that's not clinically correct.

Maybe it's too personal, too messy, too *real*.

But it's the truth.

Helping others has become the way I still love him.

The way I still feel connected.

The way I keep myself from drowning in the guilt that maybe, just maybe, I missed something. That I should have known more. Seen more. *Done* more.

And even though I know that line of thinking is cruel and unfair—I still struggle to forgive myself.

I don't have a tidy ending to this part of the story.

I'm still living it.

Still holding both the privilege of helping others and the ache of not being able to help *him*.

But this I do know:

If I can make someone feel less alone in their pain...

If I can help someone stay...

If I can use my voice so someone else doesn't feel silenced...

Then maybe that's how I honor his memory.

Maybe that's how I keep the promise I never got to make.

The Weight of Questions

During my second master's program in Counseling, I volunteered at a sexual assault crisis center. I facilitated groups for adolescent teens who had been sexually abused and separate groups for their parents. That experience shaped me in profound ways—personally and professionally. It forced me to confront the stark realities of trauma and the ripple effects it creates—not just for the survivor, but for their family, their community, and their sense of safety in the world.

A moment from one of those groups still sits heavy in my chest. We were sitting in circle, processing what it meant to share their stories, and a teen quietly said: *"It was worse after I told."*

Time slowed. My heart dropped. What hit harder was the murmur of agreement around the room.

They all nodded.

These were not girls who had kept their trauma hidden. They had spoken. They had sought help. And yet, what they found in return was not healing—it was more pain.

And then there was me.

The girl who never told.

I sat there with my silence—my untold story—face-to-face with these teens who had taken the brave step to speak, only to find out that bravery sometimes came with collateral damage. And I couldn't stop thinking: *How do we tell survivors it's safe to speak, when so often, it's not?*

The System Often Fails the Brave

If you've never looked closely at the injustices woven into the systems meant to support survivors of sexual assault, let me offer you a glimpse. Survivors are often met with disbelief, victim-blaming, or institutional failures that retraumatize them. Many are removed from their homes, schools, or support systems and placed into settings that feel clinical, unfamiliar, or unsafe—shelters, foster care, courtrooms. Meanwhile, perpetrators often face minimal consequences—if any.

As clinicians, we're taught to encourage disclosure. But when the world isn't set up to receive that disclosure with care and protection, it feels irresponsible to say, "Speak your truth," without also advocating for the systems that need to change.

That's why I take a trauma-informed approach.

What It Means to Be Trauma-Informed

To be trauma-informed is to prioritize safety, empowerment, and choice. It means understanding that trauma doesn't just live in the mind—it lives in the nervous system, the body, the behaviors we call "coping," and the silence we carry.

In trauma work, you meet people who respond in a million different ways.

Some hide.

Some sexualize themselves.

Some dissociate.

Some act out.

Some retreat into perfectionism or rage or numbness.

None of it is wrong.

It's survival.

And that's what we forget when we ask survivors questions that shame them, questions that demand clarity before trust has even been earned.

The Impact of Questions

Questions matter.

They can open a door—or slam it shut.

They can invite healing—or reinforce shame.

We need to talk about the weight of the questions we ask survivors. Because even well-intentioned questions, when asked from the wrong lens, can wound deeper than silence.

Below are examples of **traumatizing questions**—and why they hurt:

"Why didn't you just leave?"
This is often asked of those who've experienced abuse or domestic violence. It assumes that leaving is a simple, logical choice—when in reality, it's a complex and dangerous decision.

If it were easy, they would have.

Leaving can mean risking your life, your children, your financial safety, your housing, and sometimes your sanity. Survivors often stay because leaving would make things worse. That's not weakness. That's calculation.

A better question: *"What made it feel unsafe to leave?"*

"Are you sure that really happened?"
This question invalidates the survivor's experience. It implies confusion, exaggeration, or dishonesty—none of which belong in a trauma-informed conversation.

You're not an investigator.

You don't need all the facts to offer empathy.

Just listen. Believe. Support.

"What's wrong with you?"
This question assumes the person is broken, rather than responding to a broken experience.

We all think it sometimes—we just don't say it out loud.

A better way to frame curiosity is: *"What happened that made you feel this way?"* or *"Can you help me understand what you're carrying right now?"*

"Why can't you just get over it?"

Healing is not linear. This question suggests there's a deadline for pain, or that lingering trauma is a flaw.

Don't say this. Ever.

Even in your mind.

"What did you do to cause it?"

This is one of the most dangerous and shame-inducing questions we can ask. It shifts blame to the survivor and keeps them stuck in a loop of self-blame and silence.

No one *causes* abuse.

No one *invites* trauma.

Period.

"Can you tell me exactly what happened?"

Unless you're their therapist or they've invited you in, this is too much.

Recounting trauma can be retraumatizing—especially when done on someone else's timeline.

Instead, ask: *"Would you feel safe sharing part of your story with me?"* or *"I'm here when you're ready—no rush, no pressure."*

"Why are you still upset about that?"

This question minimizes trauma. It assumes that time heals all wounds—which simply isn't true.

Instead of minimizing, try curiosity: *"You seem upset—can I sit with you in that for a minute?"*

Holding Space Over Having Answers

Whether you're a clinician, a partner, a friend, or simply someone who wants to do better—know this:

You don't need the perfect words.

You don't need to fix it.

You just need to be safe.

Creating space where people feel seen, heard, and validated is more powerful than any advice you could give. That is what trauma-informed care is. That is what being human is.

If we want to heal ourselves and each other, it starts with how we speak.

How we ask.

How we listen.

We don't need to walk in someone else's shoes to walk *with* them. Empathy doesn't require agreement—it requires presence.

And that, more than anything, is what survivors need.

Words That Wound
Understanding the Weight of Traumatizing Statements

Certain words land like a punch to the gut.

They don't always come from cruelty—sometimes, they come from misunderstanding, ignorance, or even an attempt to help. But regardless of intention, traumatizing statements can strike the very core of someone who is already carrying invisible wounds.

Trauma is deeply individual. What feels neutral to one person might shatter another. Words can trigger painful memories, re-open emotional wounds, or reinforce the shame that trauma so often creates. And when those words come from someone we love—or someone in a position of trust—the pain cuts deeper.

This chapter is not about censorship.

It's about awareness.

It's about recognizing the impact of language and learning how to show up with empathy, curiosity, and care.

Personal Reflection

As a therapist, I thought I understood grief. I had read the books, taught the coping strategies, held space for countless people in pain. But when I lost my brother, everything I *thought* I knew about grief fell apart.

The grief didn't show up in stages. It showed up in waves. In silence. In rage. In the ache of unanswered questions.

What surprised me most was how often it was *my patients*—not my peers—who gave me grace. They reminded me that healing is not a linear process and that being human didn't disqualify me from being their therapist. If anything, it made me more real. More present.

But even now, years later, certain questions still knock the wind out of me.

Whenever someone asks, *"How many siblings do you have?"*—I freeze.

I say, "I'm one of six," hoping the conversation ends there. But it never does.

"Are you all close?"

And then I have to choose: lie, deflect, or re-live the loss.

Real-Life Examples of Traumatizing Statements

Here are some of the most common statements that can feel deeply invalidating, accompanied by real-life examples—both mine and those shared with me.

1. Invalidation

"Were you really that close to him?"

After my brother died, a family member made the statement that they had a closer relationship with him than I did—as if that somehow meant I didn't deserve to grieve the way I was. Grief is not a competition. Pain doesn't need to be justified.

2. Blame and Shame

"It's your fault."

Blaming a survivor only reinforces the guilt and shame

they already carry. And it tells them they were somehow responsible for something done *to* them.

3. Denial of Reality
"That didn't happen."
This statement invalidates a person's lived experience and creates emotional chaos. It's gaslighting in its purest form.

4. Insensitive Questions
"Why didn't you see the signs?"
This kind of question turns tragedy into personal failure. Survivors of suicide, abuse, or betrayal often carry the unbearable question of "what did I miss?" They don't need it reinforced by others.

5. Minimization
"Other people have it worse."
This creates a hierarchy of suffering that serves no one. Pain is not a contest. You don't need to earn your trauma.

6. Triggering Language
Certain words or phrases—especially those that echo a traumatic event—can bring back vivid flashbacks or body memories. Be aware of the language you use, especially when you know someone has experienced trauma.

7. Disbelief
"I don't believe you."
There are few things more damaging than being disbelieved when you've shared something vulnerable. It reinforces secrecy, shame, and isolation.

8. Comparisons
"At least your trauma wasn't as bad as… "
No one's healing journey is made easier by comparison. These comments rarely comfort and often deepen the sense of alienation.

9. **Forced Disclosure**
   "Tell me exactly what happened."
   Pressuring someone to share their trauma on *your* timeline is invasive. You're not entitled to their story just because you're curious—or even because you care.

10. **Lack of Empathy**
    "Get over it."
    Healing doesn't happen on demand. Dismissive responses like this send the message that someone's pain is inconvenient.

Navigating Sensitivity in Conversation

You don't have to be a therapist to be trauma-informed. You just have to be *aware*.

Here are a few alternatives that foster connection rather than disconnection:

"I'm here for you if you ever want to talk."
"Your feelings make sense."
"I may not understand, but I care."
"You don't have to explain anything if you're not ready."

Sometimes, it's not about knowing the "right" thing to say. It's about saying *less*, and listening *more*.

Creating a Culture of Empathy

Words are powerful.
   They echo long after they're spoken.
   Sometimes we carry them in our bodies for years—looping, repeating, carving stories into our self-worth.
   Whether uplifting or damaging, words shape how we see ourselves. That's why it's crucial to use them wisely—especially when speaking to someone who's hurting.

As Maya Angelou said:
*"People will forget what you said. People will forget what you did.
But people will never forget how you made them feel."*

So, the next time you're faced with someone else's pain, pause.
Reflect.
Lead with care.
Not every wound is visible—but every word has the power to
either reopen it . . . or begin the process of healing.

Chapter 4
HALF-LOVED, HALF-ME

More than anything, I wanted to be liked.

Not just socially accepted—*liked*. Approved of. Picked. Wanted. I didn't know then that it wasn't actually about popularity or being the favorite. It was about safety.

It was about survival.

It was about *abandonment*.

That wound runs deep—and when it's left unhealed, it doesn't just sit quietly. It runs the show.

Even the *threat* of being abandoned was enough to make me shift. I'd scan the room—the relationship, the friendship — and ask: "What version of me is safest here?" And that's the one I would become.

I didn't lie. I didn't pretend to be someone totally different. But I *edited* myself. I shared the light, funny, capable parts. The helpful parts. The palatable parts. The rest? The anxious, intuitive, intense, grief-filled parts? I tucked them away. Because if they saw *all* of me, they might leave. And I didn't think I could survive being left.

So, I stayed.

In relationships where I was always the giver. In friendships where my loyalty was taken for granted. In spaces that were never really safe—just familiar. I twisted myself into someone likable and useful but not fully *known*.

And there's a special kind of loneliness that comes from being half-loved. Because it affirms the worst fear: *Maybe the whole me isn't lovable at all.*

There was a chapter in my life that I now call my "partying era." From the outside, it looked like freedom. Rebellion. Letting loose. But if I'm honest, it was another mask—just with glitter and vodka.

It was connection through chaos.

It was numbing dressed up as confidence.

It was trauma meeting trauma and calling it fun.

That time came with its own pain, its own set of regrets and scars. But it also gave me something else: lived experience. And that experience became the soil where a new kind of empathy could grow.

Helping others through the same patterns—the abandonment wounds, the masking, the half-love—has been one of the most healing parts of my work. Not because I've figured it all out, but because I *see them*. I *know* what it's like to trade authenticity for attachment.

And every time I help someone name that pattern, loosen its grip, or step closer to their whole self—it heals a part of me, too.

This is the truth I've come to learn:

When you shape-shift to be liked, you teach people how to love your mask. But when you stand as your full, messy, sacred self—the ones who stay? They love *you*.

And that's the only kind of love worth keeping.

Relationships & Friendships Through a Trauma Lens

When the Mask Meets the Mirror

I looked at you and felt nothing.
You were a stranger.
Maybe you've always been one.
Maybe it was just the fantasy of you.
But the reality of you blew.
I'm shocked at the amount of energy I spent
Dreaming of you, replaying everything in my mind,
Obsessing over us and what could be.
To finally see you in person, years later, and—
I looked at you and felt nothing.
And in that moment,
I could finally set you free.

How Trauma Distorts Our Relationships

Relationships—whether romantic, platonic, or familial—are meant to be a space of connection, trust, and mutual care. But when you've experienced trauma, they often become arenas for survival, not safety.

It stops being about love and becomes about control.

About proving your worth.

About avoiding abandonment at all costs.

Trauma creates patterns. It whispers, "Don't trust too quickly. Don't get too close. Don't let them see too much." It teaches us to perform instead of connect, to monitor instead of feel. And so, we armor up—behind kindness, behind silence, behind perfectionism—hoping it'll protect us from being hurt again.

But the armor becomes the mask. And the mask becomes the relationship.

Common Trauma Patterns in Relationships

Trust and Vulnerability: The Double-Edged Sword

Difficulty Trusting: Even when people show up, trauma tells us to stay guarded.

Fear of Being Real: Authenticity once came at a cost—rejection, ridicule, abandonment.

Hyper-Independence vs. Codependency: We swing between "I don't need anyone" and "please don't leave me." Survival doesn't leave much room for middle ground.

REALITY CHECK:
Your nervous system isn't broken—it's responding to what it learned. Healing doesn't mean blindly trusting everyone. It means learning to discern who is safe—and who is not.

Communication and Boundaries: The Struggle is Real

Struggling to Speak Up: We learned to prioritize others' comfort over our own truth.

Boundary Guilt: "No" used to come with consequences—now it comes with guilt.

Overexplaining: Because somewhere along the way, "no" stopped being enough. We learned we had to earn our space with justification.

REALITY CHECK:
Boundaries don't push the right people away—they show you who respects you enough to stay. Having good boundaries is a form of self-respect, and the people who resist our boundaries the most are the ones who have been benefiting from our lack of boundaries.

Triggers in Relationships: When the Past Hijacks the Present

Hypervigilance: Every delayed text or offhand comment feels like a warning sign.

Emotional Flashbacks: A minor rejection can trigger a storm of old pain.

Overanalysis: Because last time we missed a red flag, and we refuse to miss it again.

REALITY CHECK:
Sometimes people are just tired, distracted, or imperfect. But when you've lived in a state of survival, everything feels like a potential threat.

Elementary School: The Mask of Joy

I was the bubbly one—the Girl Scout, the star student, the achiever. But behind the smile:
- A backpack hidden so it wouldn't smell like smoke.
- Chronic stomachaches from silent anxiety.
- A name on the classroom sheet with no parent listed.
- The father-daughter dance . . . without my father.

Even then, I learned that love could disappear. That attention could sting. That being overlooked would shape how I saw myself—and how I let others treat me.

High School: The Collapse

Returning to Fond du Lac, Wisconsin, in 10th grade felt like entering someone else's movie halfway through.

- I had a new last name, a rewritten past.
- I re-entered a friend group now drowning in drugs—and I went with them.
- A car accident I wasn't even in somehow became "my fault."
- Friends turned on me. Isolation wrapped in silence.

It was abandonment all over again—just dressed in different clothes.

Fantasy vs. Reality in Love and Friendship

When I didn't know how to trust people, I learned to imagine them instead.

- In my mind, they were loyal, supportive, kind.
- In real life, they were inconsistent, withholding, cold.

I believed:
- Love meant proving myself—again and again.
- Friendships meant overgiving and expecting little.
- Boundaries meant loss.

But here's the truth:
- Love doesn't require exhaustion.
- Friendships should be reciprocal.
- Boundaries aren't rejection—they're protection.

REALITY CHECK:
If someone only loves the high-energy, always-available version of you—but not the quiet, tired, or overwhelmed parts—they don't love you. They love your performance.

Trauma Bonds & Abandonment Wounds

In my twenties, I didn't have the language for trauma bonds. I just knew this:
- If I overgave, maybe they'd stay.
- If I abandoned myself, maybe I wouldn't be abandoned by others.
- If I kept the peace, maybe I wouldn't be punished.

But eventually, I learned:
- Trauma bonds aren't love—they're survival.
- Chasing people who breadcrumb you is a reenactment, not a relationship.
- You don't have to earn love through pain.

The Relationship That Broke Me

I didn't want marriage until I met him. He pointed at an old couple holding hands and said, "That'll be us one day." He made me believe in forever.

And then he left.

The grief became physical. I couldn't eat. I couldn't sleep. I moved through life like a ghost, trying to hold myself together in a world that suddenly didn't make sense.

I had uprooted my life for him—moved cities, shifted careers, sacrificed stability. And in the end, I was left with a broken heart and a locked door I've been trying to reopen ever since.

Final Reflections: Breaking the Pattern

- Love that demands your silence, your exhaustion, or your disappearance is not love.
- People who leave when you set boundaries were only there for the version of you who didn't have any.
- You are not too much. You were simply too honest for the wrong people.

You deserve connection that feels safe—not performative. You deserve friendships that don't come with strings or conditions. You deserve to rest, to be seen, to be loved—not for the mask you wear, but for the truth of who you are beneath it.

And in case no one told you today: You are worthy of love that doesn't make you question your worth.

Chapter 5

THE COST OF THE MASK

Wearing the mask worked—until it didn't.

And by the time it stopped working, the damage had already woven itself into every corner of my life.

The truth is, masking doesn't just hide you from others—it hides you from yourself. You start forgetting what's real and what's performative. You say you're "fine" so often, you start believing it. You confuse achievement with healing. You confuse being needed with being loved.

On the outside, I was the strong one. The therapist. The friend who always showed up. The overachiever. The reliable one.

But internally? I was exhausted. Disconnected. Anxious. Deeply lonely—even when surrounded by people. Because no one could truly see me. And how could they? I didn't let them.

The impact of masking and unaddressed trauma didn't just touch my personal life—it ran through my relationships, my health, my work, my body.

- I stayed in relationships that mirrored my trauma because I didn't trust my instincts.

- I overextended myself to the point of burnout, thinking if I did more, I'd finally *feel* more.

- I disconnected from my body—ignoring signals, suppressing emotions, bypassing pain in the name of "being okay."

- I couldn't rest. I didn't know how. Rest felt like failure.

The mask told me to keep going. To keep fixing. To keep performing. But all that energy spent on appearing okay meant I never learned how to *be* okay.

I see now that masking is a survival tool—not a life plan.

It may protect you for a while, but it will cost you connection, creativity, peace, and joy. It will keep you chasing worth instead of embodying it. It will trick you into thinking your value comes from what you *do*, not who you *are*.

And maybe the worst part?

You get so used to shrinking yourself to be digestible… that you forget how to take up space as your whole self.

That's the real impact of the mask. It doesn't just silence your pain—it muffles your power. And this book—this work—is the process of reclaiming both.

Trust from a Traumatized Lens

When Safety Is a Memory, Not a Feeling

Trust is one of the most fragile things to rebuild after trauma. When it's been broken—by people, systems, or by the ways we've abandoned ourselves to survive—it leaves a mark that is more than emotional. It becomes physiological. The nervous system learns to expect harm, even when nothing threatening is happening. What should feel safe instead feels suspicious. Peace feels unfamiliar. Rest becomes uncomfortable.

Rebuilding trust isn't just about learning to trust *others* again—it's about learning to trust *yourself*. Your instincts. Your inner voice. The gut feelings you silenced to survive. The people you held on to for too long. The moments you ignored red flags because peace felt too foreign to trust.

Sometimes we get so good at adapting to a room that we forget how to belong in one.

Why Trust Feels Impossible After Trauma

1. Loss of Safety: When Trust Is Violated

- **Betrayal Cuts Deep**
  Trauma often begins with betrayal—by someone we loved, a place we thought was safe, or a system that promised to protect us.

- **A Shattered Worldview**
  What we believed about the world—fairness, safety, good intentions—suddenly collapses. Everything becomes uncertain, unstable, unsafe.

Reflection: Rebuilding trust isn't about choosing to trust. It's about retraining the nervous system to believe it's safe. Emotional healing and physiological safety go hand in hand.

2. Walls We Build: Protection or Isolation?

- **Suspicion of Goodness**
  Even when someone shows up with consistency and care, the trauma brain whispers, "Don't fall for it. It won't last."

- **The Pull Toward Isolation**
  Distance feels safer than closeness. Not because we don't care, but because intimacy feels like a risk we can't afford.

Reflection: Isolation may protect you from disappointment, but it also robs you of the healing that connection offers. You deserve both protection and companionship.

3. Trusting Yourself Again

- **Self-Betrayal and Shame**
  "I should have known better." "Why did I stay?" "Why didn't

I speak up?" These thoughts become a looping narrative of self-doubt.

- **Reconnecting to Your Intuition**
  You didn't fail—you adapted. You did what you needed to do to survive. And survival is not weakness—it's strength.

Reflection: Every time you ignored your instincts, it was for a reason. Now, with more tools and awareness, you can start listening again. That's the foundation of self-trust.

How to Rebuild Trust (Without Gaslighting Yourself)

1. Start Small: Create Internal Safety

- **Build Predictability**
  Trauma thrives in chaos. Stability—through routines, rituals, or even a consistent bedtime—helps rewire your nervous system.

- **Honor Your Boundaries**
  Set limits with others and with yourself. Give yourself permission to say, "I deserve to feel safe here."

Reflection: Boundaries may feel unnatural at first, especially if you've always been the one to keep the peace. But boundaries are the beginning of trust.

2. Relearn Your Intuition

- **What Was I Sensing Back Then?**
  Go back and explore the moments you silenced your gut. What did your body know before your mind caught up?

- **You Did What You Had To Do**
  Sometimes survival means ignoring what we know. Now, you can listen with a different level of awareness and safety.

Reflection: You won't trust your intuition overnight. But every small moment of listening—every time you honor a red flag or follow your gut—is progress.

3. Healing Happens in Safe Relationships

- **Not Everyone Deserves Your Trust—But Someone Does**
  The work isn't about trusting everyone. It's about learning who can hold that space with you.

- **Therapy Helps—So Does Connection**
  A friend who truly listens. A partner who honors your boundaries. A mentor who sees your worth. These people help rewrite the story.

Reflection: If you haven't found those people yet, don't give up. They exist. And you weren't meant to heal alone.

Personal Reflection: Trust Is a Long Game

Even now, I struggle with trust in my personal life. As a therapist, I know how to hold space, offer compassion, and create safety for others. But in my own relationships? That's where things still feel tender.

When I've tried to show up as my full self—raw, open, vulnerable—I've too often been met with blank stares or performative concern. Or worse, responses that diminish what I've just risked sharing.

Statements like:
- "Well, that happened to me too. "
- "You're just being too sensitive."
- "You're overreacting."

Those comments don't just sting—they shut me down. My body remembers. And I retreat. Not out of choice, but out of survival.

That's why writing has become sacred. Here, I get to say what's real. I get to speak without interruption, without performance, without needing to make it more palatable. I get to be Kaitlyn—messy, whole, unfinished.

And each time I do, it gets a little easier. That's how I know I'm healing.

Final Reflections: Reclaiming Trust

- Trust isn't a light switch—it's a muscle.

- You don't owe trust to anyone who hasn't earned it.

- But you *do* owe yourself the opportunity to feel safe again.

- You are allowed to move slowly.

- You are allowed to vet people.

- You are allowed to walk away.

You don't need to be fearless to begin again. You just need to be willing.

Part Two

THE BODY, THE BREAK, THE BECOMING

Chapter 6

THE SLOW BECOMING

Healing didn't happen all at once. There was no single breakthrough moment, no dramatic scene where everything clicked into place. My journey unfolded slowly—in layers, in spirals, in relapses and returns. It was less like climbing a mountain and more like learning to live in my own body again. Reconnecting and healing the nervous system.

At first, I didn't know I was healing—I just knew I couldn't keep living the way I was.

So, I started small. I gave myself permission to feel what I had spent years suppressing. In order to heal, we have to feel—I tell my patients this all the time. I let the tears come. I got angry. I grieved. Truthfully, until my brother died, I had only cried like two times a year; and it was only for a brief moment. When he passed, the flood gates opened as if the tears were backlogged, and I couldn't stop them. I stopped numbing and started noticing. I began to unlearn the belief that I had to earn rest, or love, or safety. I started choosing relationships where I didn't have to perform. I sat in therapy not as the clinician, but as the human. The sister. The woman who was tired of being strong.

I began to build a life that didn't require a mask.

I listened to my body—not just when it was in crisis, but daily. I honored my sensory needs, my boundaries, my need for structure and regulation. I practiced being present, even when it was uncomfortable. I said "no," more often. I allowed myself to be seen—really seen—by people who loved me, not just for what I could give, but for who I was.

I used the same tools I'd taught others: Mindfulness. Nervous system regulation. Cognitive reframing. Self-compassion. But now, I let them *land.* I let them transform *me.*

And I leaned into my autistic identity—not as a limitation, but as a guidepost. It showed me how to live a life that actually fit.

Healing didn't make me invincible. I still have triggers. I still have off days. I still carry the imprint of trauma. But I'm not trapped by it anymore.

I no longer live *for* the mask. I live for the moments of real connection. For the quiet mornings where I'm not performing. For the work that aligns with my values. For the people who meet me where I'm at—not where I pretend to be.

That's what healing gave me:

Not perfection.

But presence.

Not control.

But choice.

And that's how I started building a better life—one decision at a time.

Grief Trauma—The Interwoven Tapestry of Grief and Trauma

When Grief and Trauma Collide

Grief and trauma are often spoken about as separate experiences—grief as sorrow, trauma as fear. But for many of us, they arrive together. Grief is the natural response to loss. Trauma complicates that grief by disrupting our sense of safety, our identity, and our ability to process the loss at all. When these two forces meet, the result is an overwhelming emotional and physical storm that changes you—sometimes permanently.

My Grief Journey

"I feel so lost. I didn't just lose you—I lost myself. I don't feel connected to anyone. I can't be who I once was because I don't know who she is. Did I ever know? It all feels like smoke and mirrors. Nothing is real, and once that bubble of delusion is popped, there is no way to go back."

This is how I described the aftermath of my brother's death in one of my journal entries. The moment I lost him, everything

shifted. My identity, my purpose, my understanding of the world—
it all collapsed. Grief has a way of stripping away the illusions we
hold about ourselves and the roles we play. I wasn't just grieving
him. I was grieving the version of myself that died with him.

There's a unique kind of loneliness that emerges when your
identity is shaken by loss. I didn't recognize the woman staring
back at me in the mirror. I was no longer the "fun" one. I couldn't
laugh it off, drink it away, or hustle through the pain. I couldn't
return to the person I used to be—because that version of me
didn't know how to survive this kind of sorrow.

The Guilt That Lingers

Being around people who couldn't even say the word "suicide"
made the grief feel heavier. It was as if the truth of what happened
to my brother needed to be hidden, erased, buried. But how can
we heal when the reality of our loss is treated like a secret?

I carried guilt that didn't belong to me but felt impossible to
release. I knew logically that I wasn't responsible. But my heart
didn't believe it. Every interaction, every missed sign, played on
repeat in my mind. The shame was suffocating.

When Grief Threatens Purpose

In the depths of that grief, I almost shut down my private practice.
I questioned everything—my purpose, my capacity to help others,
my ability to keep going. I had also decided not to publish my
first book. It felt impossible to write about healing when I could
barely get out of bed.

And then, I had a dream. In it, I was given wings. Whether it
came from the universe or from my brother, it felt like a sign I
couldn't ignore. That dream reminded me that even when we are
lost in darkness, there's something calling us forward.

My patients were another lifeline. Their grace, their empathy,
their presence—it all helped me stay grounded. They reminded
me that healing is never one-sided. We hold space for each other.
We show up to each other. And in those shared moments of connection, we both heal.

Grief: The Weight of Loss

Grief is never just emotional. It lives in the body, in the nervous system, in the fatigue that won't go away. For me, grief felt like a weight in my chest that made it hard to breathe, to focus, to move.

Grief isn't always about death. It can come from the loss of a relationship, a dream, a version of yourself. It's messy. It's non-linear. And it's deeply personal.

Trauma: The Silent Disruptor

Trauma is the psychological imprint left behind when safety is shattered. It creates a ripple effect—hypervigilance, emotional numbness, disconnection from the body and others. When trauma and grief overlap, it becomes almost impossible to tease them apart.

After my brother's death, I wasn't just grieving him. I was reliving the trauma of how it happened. The loss itself was traumatic, but so was the aftermath, the silence, the shame, the systems that failed us. It felt like my grief was stuck in a time loop. I couldn't move forward because trauma had frozen me in place.

The Grief Tsunami

Grief doesn't move in a straight line. It ebbs and flows. One day you laugh. The next, you're on the floor, consumed by guilt for that moment of joy. There's a duality that no one prepares you for—being alive in a world where someone you love no longer exists.

Anniversaries amplify it. Every August, I feel the weight of my brother's death as if it just happened. My mind replays scenarios—what I could have done differently, how I might have saved him. I fantasize about trading places. I volunteer as "tribute." But none of it changes the truth. He's gone. And I'm still here.

The Mask I Could No Longer Wear

After my brother died, I couldn't perform anymore. The drinking, the overworking, the "I'm fine" script—I dropped it all. Not by choice, but because it simply stopped working.

People wanted the old version of me back. The one who was bubbly, productive, agreeable. But she was gone. And pretending she wasn't felt like betrayal. Grief had stripped me bare, and all that remained was a raw, quieter version of myself—one I barely recognized.

Grief as Transformation

As I moved through the grief, something shifted. I began to see that my identity was evolving. I was no longer just Kaitlyn. I was a sister carrying the weight of loss. I was someone re-learning how to live, how to speak the truth, how to show up with vulnerability and strength.

Grief became a portal. A painful one, yes—but also a path to something deeper. Purpose. Meaning. Clarity.

The Relationship Between Grief and Trauma

When trauma is part of the loss, everything gets more complicated. Sudden death. Suicide. Violence. These things don't allow for neat stages of grief. They leave behind questions, unfinished conversations, and deep psychological wounds.

You're not just grieving the person—you're grieving the story, the circumstances, the systemic failures. You're grieving the way the world *should* have been. And that kind of grief doesn't resolve. It transforms.

Final Reflections: Keep Going

Grief and trauma change you. They dismantle who you were and invite you to become someone new. That process is not clean. It's not linear. And it certainly isn't fast.

But it's real. And it's possible.

This chapter isn't just about pain—it's about what happens when you walk through the pain instead of around it. It's about staying in the arena when everything inside you wants to run. It's about honoring the person you lost without losing yourself in the process.

To anyone navigating grief and trauma:

You are not alone.

You are not broken.

You are being reshaped.

Keep going.

Chapter 7

NUMBING THE PAIN

By the time I experienced trauma in adulthood, I was already a master at surviving. I had decades of practice—masking, achieving, people-pleasing, pushing through. But survival has limits. And when the pain got too big, I stopped trying to manage it. I started trying to escape it.

The death of my brother was the breaking point. It wasn't just grief—it was devastation. It wasn't just sadness—it was guilt, shock, rage, confusion, and a kind of sorrow that settled into my bones. It felt unbearable. And I didn't have the tools to fully carry it. Although I taught others the tools (as a clinician), I found it hard to apply them to myself. It felt like a double-edged sword. Connections that weren't real. And a mask that said, "I'm fine."

People don't always recognize that numbing is its own trauma response. It's not weakness. It's not failure. It's the body's desperate attempt to *survive* the unbearable. Forgetting the ache in my chest. Forgetting the weight of trying to hold everyone else together. Forgetting that I had lost someone I loved more than life, and I couldn't bring him back—no matter how many people I helped.

Grief made the mask feel exposed.

But it also made me real.

Because eventually, the numbing didn't work anymore. The hurt started lasting longer than the relief. The nights out felt more hollow. And the voice inside me—the one I had buried for years—started to speak again.

I wish I could say I just woke up one day and chose healing. But it was slower than that. It was one painful reckoning at a time. One moment of honesty. One decision to stop running.

And when I started facing the pain—really sitting with it, really *feeling* it—I realized I wasn't just grieving my brother. I was grieving *everything* I'd lost while trying to be someone I wasn't.

My writing really saved me, and I slowly accepted that the

mask had to come off. Because now I have something else:
Truth.
Tools.
And the ability to sit in the dark without disappearing into it.

When Celebration Feels Like Survival

Holidays are marketed as seasons of joy, connection, and tradition. But for those carrying grief or trauma, these times of the year can feel like a cruel contrast between internal reality and external expectation. The lights are bright, the music is cheerful, and the world demands celebration—but your heart feels heavy, broken, or numb.

This chapter explores the intersection of trauma, grief, and cultural pressure during the holiday season—and how to navigate it without abandoning yourself in the process.

1. **The Holidays as a Reminder of Loss**

    - **Empty Spaces:** An unoccupied chair at the table. A name unspoken. A silence that echoes louder than laughter. The absence isn't just symbolic—it's palpable.

    - **Unmet Expectations:** The world offers a curated image of holidays—warm, connected, full of joy. When your inner world doesn't match, it can feel like you're failing at something you never signed up for.

2. **Social Pressure vs. Isolation**

    - **Performing Happiness:** Even in the depths of pain, there's an expectation to show up, smile, participate. For many, this is exhausting and retraumatizing.

- **Withdrawing to Survive:** Avoiding gatherings can feel like self-preservation, but it can also create a deeper sense of isolation. The challenge becomes finding a middle ground—enough connection to feel supported, enough space to feel safe.

3. Nostalgia & Triggers

- **Bittersweet Memories:** Holidays are a time capsule. They bring back moments we cherish—and moments we'd rather forget.

- **Unseen Triggers:** A familiar smell. A family recipe. A Christmas carol. Trauma lives in the body, and sometimes the most ordinary things bring back extraordinary pain.

4. Coping Mechanisms—Healthy & Unhealthy

- **Numbing:** When the emotional weight is too much, it's tempting to turn to alcohol, food, or avoidance. While these offer temporary relief, they often deepen the pain in the long run.

- **Withdrawal:** Not showing up at all can feel easier—but complete disconnecting can make the grief louder. Coping doesn't mean pretending. It means making space for what's real.

5. Support Systems—Or Lack Thereof

- **Misunderstood Grief:** One of the hardest things is grieving in a room full of people who don't understand. Even a well-meaning family can say the wrong thing—or say nothing at all.

- **The Power of Empathy:** You don't need someone to fix it. You just need someone to witness it. Being seen, being heard, being allowed to grieve without judgment—that's real support.

6. Cultural & Religious Considerations

- **Grief Across Traditions:** In some cultures, grief is honored during holidays through rituals and remembrance. In others, there's pressure to suppress it. Recognizing your own needs—and honoring your grief in ways that feel authentic—can be a powerful act of self-respect.

7. Seeking Professional Support

- **Therapy:** Holidays often stir up unresolved wounds. Having a safe, therapeutic space guided by a trained professional can help you explore those reactions with more clarity and compassion.

- **Community:** Grief and support groups remind us we're not the only ones feeling fractured during this time of year. Even one shared story can make you feel less alone.

Personal Refection: My First Holiday Without Him

Maybe someone's already written about it. Maybe there are guides or essays or posts that try to prepare you. But I hadn't seen one that told the truth.

That first holiday after loss? It wrecked me.

The first "celebration" after my brother died was his birthday. It was too soon—raw and chaotic—but people showed up. They tried. We were all still pretending we were okay. But Thanksgiving? That was different. The room was quieter. The absence, louder.

I convinced myself I'd be fine. That I'd celebrate for him. That

I'd stay busy and push through. I did the Turkey Trot run like I always do, but it felt surreal, like I wasn't really in my body.

Then I checked a group chat and saw someone joking about their kids pretending their brother had died. Everyone laughed. I didn't. It felt like a gut punch. Like the air had been sucked out of the day. I couldn't believe how careless people could be with something that felt so sacred to me.

My husband, trying his best, wore a full turkey costume. He was doing everything he could to lighten the mood. But I was spiraling. I was there—but not really. Grief had taken over.

That was the day I finally understood my cousin, who stopped showing up after her father passed. Holidays change. Families change. You change.

And nothing, no tradition, no performance—can undo the truth of what's missing.

The Dysfunction of It All

The holidays are often dysfunctional to begin with. Add in grief or trauma, and the dysfunction becomes unbearable.

There are videos online now encouraging people to skip forced family events, and honestly—I'm here for it. Why do we keep pushing ourselves into spaces filled with unresolved pain, alcohol, and expectations to smile through it?

Now, in my late thirties, the holidays feel less like a celebration and more like a battlefield. The older I get, the heavier the silence becomes. The pressure to perform. The pain of pretending.

And I'm tired.

I'm tired of smiling when my chest aches.

Tired of small talk that ignores what's real.

Tired of trying to protect other people's comfort while I abandon my own truth.

So this year, I'm choosing something else.

No more gatherings that steal my peace.

No more masks to make others feel okay.

No more sacrificing myself in the name of tradition.

Because now I have to ask: who was I really doing all this for?

Final Reflections: Grief Strips Away the Noise

After the initial shock fades, and after I stopped using alcohol to dull the edges, what I was left with was silence.

And in that silence—I miss him.

Last Christmas, I begged for a sign. A rainbow appeared in the sky.

This year, I'll be looking again. Not because it erases the pain. But because it reminds me he's still with me, even if everything else has changed.

Chapter 8

TURNING POINTS

There came a point in my healing where I realized I had all the tools—I just hadn't been using them on myself.

I had the research. The education. The training. The clinical skills. I knew the theories. The models. The stages of grief. The scripts for trauma work. I could help others untangle their pain. But I had never truly applied the same care, compassion, or curiosity to *me*.

Until I did.

And that changed everything.

It started with practicing what I preach.

Sitting still. Regulating. Asking myself the same questions I pose to clients. Listening—really listening—to my own nervous system. Letting myself feel. Letting myself *need*.

I stopped hiding behind my credentials and started *living* what I knew. Not perfectly. Not all at once. But consistently. Gently. Honestly.

And then something shifted even deeper.

I began to tell my story.

Not for pity. Not to overshare. But because I *needed* to. And because I saw what happened when I did.

The first time I told a patient about my brother's passing, I was terrified. Clinicians are taught to be neutral, contained, professional. But in that moment, I chose *human* first.

And something profound happened.

The person sitting across from me softened. They breathed differently. They felt seen. Because suddenly, this wasn't just therapy—it was connection. It was real.

In sharing my story—in letting my pain breathe in the room—I didn't just honor my brother's memory. I kept him *alive* in a way that continues to ripple. And I believe, with everything in me, that doing so has helped others who might've been feeling what he once felt—that silent, crushing weight of being *too much* and not *enough* all at once.

Telling the truth didn't just help my clients. It helped *me*.

It let me be whole in the room. Not a clinician with answers, but a human with *honest presence*.

That was the real turning point.

When I stopped using my knowledge to *distance* myself from my pain, and started using it to *move toward* it.

When I stopped hiding behind the mask of the professional, and started showing up—raw, real, regulated enough—to sit in the mess with others.

That's when healing became sacred. Not just a process. But a *purpose*.

The Art of Trauma—Expressive Pathways to Healing and Understanding

Turning Pain into Expression, and Expression into Power

The "art of trauma" lives at the intersection of suffering and self-expression. For many survivors, creativity becomes the place where the unspeakable is finally spoken—through brushstrokes, through rhythm, through words. Art becomes a refuge, a reclamation, and often, an act of defiance.

In this chapter, we explore how creative expression supports healing, connection, and transformation. Whether through storytelling, visual art, movement, or ritual, the act of creating becomes a vital part of making sense of pain—and making meaning from it.

1. Expressive Arts and Trauma

- **Art as a Healing Tool**
  Trauma often lives beyond language. Art bridges that gap. It provides a non-verbal pathway for processing overwhelming emotions and surfacing buried memories.

- **Art Therapy as Sanctuary**
  In clinical spaces, art therapy offers a structured, safe
  environment to explore trauma with fewer cognitive
  defenses. Through drawing, movement, or sculpture,
  survivors re-engage their nervous systems with gentleness and curiosity.

2. Artistic Expression as Advocacy

- **Art as Platform**
  Survivors often use their creative work to challenge
  stigma, share truth, and spark social change. Their stories create waves far beyond the page or canvas.

- **Storytelling That Connects**
  Memoirs. Documentaries. Spoken word. These forms
  remind others that they're not alone in their grief, fear, or
  rage. Art not only bears witness—it builds bridges.

*When I share the art of healing—the art of trauma—it feels less
isolating. It creates connection. And after all, what else are we here
to do?*

3. The Power of Storytelling in Healing

- **Writing as Release**
  Journaling, poetry, or narrative writing offers structure
  to emotional chaos. It turns pain into language—and that
  language makes space for clarity, even if the clarity is
  messy.

- **Visual Storytelling**
  Illustration, photography, or comics can capture what
  words cannot. These mediums bypass the logical brain
  and speak directly to feeling.

4. **Cultural Exploration and Trauma**

- **Art as Cultural Memory**
  Across cultures, storytelling, ritual, and visual art are used to process intergenerational trauma. These practices preserve identity while giving voice to stories that were never allowed to be told.

- **Reclaiming Identity Through Creation**
  Art can help survivors rebuild who they are—on their own terms. It creates a new internal narrative, one that isn't defined by harm.

5. **Trauma as a Catalyst for Creation**

- **Pain as a Muse**
  Many artists create not despite their pain—but because of it. Trauma becomes the raw material for transformation.

- **Expression as Strength**
  To put emotion into form is to release what was once frozen. Creation becomes movement. And movement becomes healing.

Art is chaos. Trauma is chaotic. Healing is Messy AF.

My Personal Journey: When Trauma Became My Art

I never set out to be an author.

The most life-altering trauma I've experienced was losing my brother to suicide. I was in the process of preparing my first book when it happened. It was going to be a simple eBook. I had found a self-publishing agency. I was about to sign the contract.

And then, the phone call.

It was my cousin. We never called each other—not early in the morning.

"Have you talked to your dad?"

"No. Why?"

"Kaitlyn, there's been an accident."

"What are you talking about?"

"It's Charles. He was in an accident."

"Shut the fuck up. Are you serious?"

The ringing in my ears. The silence. The fog. I called my dad, but he couldn't speak. His neighbor took the phone.

The first words that left my mouth were:

"Was it suicide?"

Even now, writing this, my body remembers. My chest tightens. The tears come.

That moment—everything split open.

Writing as Resistance: Turning Pain into Words

People mocked my writing for years.

So, of course, I became an author. Not out of spite. Out of necessity.

Because this is how I reclaim my voice.

Let me show you my art. Let me show you my words that don't fit neurotypical grammar or cadence. My neurodivergent brain doesn't just think differently; it *speaks* differently. That difference? That's where my power lives.

I don't write for perfection. I write for impact.

I don't write to follow rules. I write to break cages.

When I released my first book, I was prepared for criticism. I expected rejection. I had been trained to believe my words were too much.

But what came back?

Resonance.

Readers didn't just understand the message. They felt it. My words were heard—not just seen.

And that moment changed me. I didn't just write to survive anymore.

I wrote to be free.

The Defiance of Healing

Healing is resistance.
Healing is rebellion.
Healing is art.
The world tells us to stay quiet, get over it, move on.
But healing doesn't follow polite timelines. It doesn't care about family dynamics or societal norms. Healing demands truth—and truth rarely shows up pretty or on schedule.
So no—don't tell me how to grieve my brother. Don't tell me how to process the trauma I didn't choose. Don't ask me to clean it up for your comfort.
Grief isn't neat.
Trauma isn't linear.
Healing isn't about return; it's about rebirth.
And that messy, spiraling, sacred process?
That *is* the art.

Personal Reflection: The Art of Healing

If I could speak to my younger self, the one sitting in shock, doubting her voice, I would tell her this:
Healing isn't about becoming who you were before the trauma. It's about *becoming someone new*, forged by pain, but not defined by it. Like a phoenix.
That's why I write.
That's why I speak.
That's why I'll keep sharing, even when my voice shakes.
Because every time I do, someone else feels less alone.
And that is the art of trauma.

The Second Time Around: Writing as an Author, Again

Being an author is a role I deeply enjoy. It's the most authentic expression of who I am—a thread of my soul woven into every page. But writing this second book? It's a completely different experience.

The first book poured out of me like a controlled burn—intense, messy, but manageable. This one? It's a purge. A relentless, gut-wrenching, soul-expelling purge. Each chapter feels like I'm unearthing buried trauma, brushing off the dust, and forcing myself to sit with it long enough to find the words.

And let's be honest, why did I choose to write the trauma chapter? I could skip it, start over, pick an easier path. But that's just not who I am.

So instead, I lean in. I pour everything I've got onto the page. Not just a little—everything.

This book doesn't come from a place of ease. It comes from the truth. From lived experience. From the willingness to go there—even when it hurts.

If you're holding these pages now, know this: You're not just reading a book. You're witnessing the process of turning pain into power.

You're welcome.

Untethering From Trauma—Or Am I?

Maybe I thought I had already untangled myself from my past—that by the time I sat down to write, I'd be detached enough to tell my story without feeling it clawing at my chest.

I was wrong.

Speaking it into existence, spelling it out letter by letter, makes it more real than I ever anticipated. Did I stuff it too close to my heart? Did I build an identity so rooted in survival that breaking it down means breaking myself in the process?

Is this the moment where the persona I created to survive crumbles?

The Writing Experience—Then vs. Now

I try to compare this writing process to my last one, but it feels like a blur. Maybe I was so consumed by my trauma the first time that I didn't have the clarity to notice the struggle.

But this time? I notice everything.

The doubt.
The overthinking.
The feeling of "Who the fuck is going to read this?"
The panic of "Does this even make sense?"
And today? The mental block is debilitating.

The story is inside me, but I can't seem to find the right way to write it.

The ideas swirl: "Do this. No, do this. No, Kaitlyn, wait, do it this way." And suddenly, I'm stuck in a tornado of over analysis, frozen in place. Is this just part of the process, or do all authors feel this way?

Struggling to Find My Voice

I want to write a coming-of-age story, but how do I shape it? How do I make it resonate? I feel alone in this process, and the garbage thoughts creep back in:

"You're not good enough."

"Who wants to listen to you?"

"Who cares?"

Those thoughts? They are the most destabilizing, most paralyzing barriers to creativity.

I remind myself that writing is a fight—one I must show up for, even when the words don't come easily.

Fully Dressed, Completely Exposed

What happens when you are trying to write
But you are literally paralyzed by the content
You are trying to spill?
I feel so exposed and I am fully dressed.
I feel like the flesh is just ripping on the inside
While the outside is composed.
No one asks if you are okay, no one asks if you need help,
Because you portray and carry it so well.
Is this a blessing or a curse?
Time will tell.

Final Reflections: The Journey Continues

Despite the doubt, despite the imposter syndrome, even though some days the words feel stuck in my throat like unspoken confessions—I keep writing.

Because the truth is, writing is the only thing that makes sense to me.

It's how I heal. It's how I take control of my story.

And even if I don't always know where the words will take me, I know I must keep going.

Chapter 9

BUILDING A LIFE WITHOUT THE MASK

Taking the mask off wasn't one big moment — it was a thousand tiny choices.

It was deciding not to laugh at something that hurt me.

It was letting myself pause before responding, instead of giving the polished, expected answer.

It was saying "I don't know" in a meeting.

It was crying in front of someone I trusted, even though every cell in my body told me not to.

It was learning to sit in stillness — and learning that stillness didn't mean failure.

The truth is that the mask didn't just fall off.

I had to *unlearn* it.

I had to build a life that no longer required it.

Here's what that looked like in practice:

1. I stopped saying "yes" out of fear.
For years, I agreed to things I didn't want to do—socially, professionally, emotionally—because I thought if I said "no," I'd lose connection. But boundaries aren't rejection. They're protection. And when I started setting them, I finally made space for *reciprocity*.

2. I gave myself permission to feel.
The mask trained me to numb. Healing taught me to feel without apology. I made room for joy, anger, grief, overstimulation, all of it—without judgment. My emotions weren't problems to fix. They were messages to listen to.

3. I honored my neurodivergence.
I stopped pretending I was "just quirky" or "bad at social stuff." I embraced structure, regulated my sensory inputs, allowed myself to stim (engage in repetitive movements or sounds that help regulate emotions or energy), and stopped overcommitting just to feel

"normal." I learned to accommodate myself—unapologetically.

4. I stopped chasing worth and started embodying it.
I no longer need to be perfect to be enough. I don't need to prove my value by over-functioning. I've built a life where I'm worthy simply because I exist—not because I perform.

5. I surrounded myself with safe people.
I used to call everyone a friend. Now, I look for resonance, not just history. I seek relationships where my full self is welcomed—not tolerated, not fixed—but *witnessed*. That kind of safety changed everything.

This life—this unmasked life—is quieter. Slower. But deeper.

There's less noise and more meaning.

Less approval-seeking, more authenticity.

And for the first time, I don't feel like I'm living for someone else's version of me.

I'm building this life one choice at a time. And with each unmasked step, I move closer to the girl in the yellow dress—the one who always knew who I was, and was just waiting for me to remember.

I didn't write this book from a pedestal—I wrote it from the inside of the healing process. I've lived the mask. I've buried my truth to survive. I've felt the weight of grief, trauma, and disconnection. And I've slowly, imperfectly, fought my way back to myself. This book isn't about perfection—it's about possibility. I've experienced real healing. And I genuinely believe that the concepts, reflections, and tools within these pages can help *you* begin or deepen your healing too. Not by becoming someone new—but by finally becoming fully, freely, *you*.

The Weight We Carry—Socioeconomic Trauma and Survival

The relationship between socioeconomic status (SES) and trauma is layered, generational, and inseparable from identity. It's not just about income, it's about how power, access, privilege, and oppression intersect to shape our realities. Trauma doesn't discriminate, but systemic inequality ensures that some of us carry more of it than others.

As Dr. Gabor Maté reminds us, "Trauma is not what happens to you. Trauma is what happens inside you as a result of what happens to you." When survival becomes your baseline, there's no space left to process. You're not failing to heal—you're too busy surviving.

This chapter is about that survival. About the resilience it takes to grow up inside broken systems, and about the cost of that resilience. It's also about reclaiming your power—through understanding, through healing, and through creating change.

When Survival Is the Only Option

Living in poverty is a trauma all its own. You become fluent in hypervigilance. You learn that anything—housing, food, relationships—can disappear without warning. There's no cushion. No net. Just you, bracing for impact.

My own socioeconomic upbringing split me in two. My mom and I walked everywhere—grocery bags in hand, dodging potholes and judgment. We didn't have a car, except for a brief period when we had "Nester the Nova," a white car my mom named with pride. A nun crashed into us in the Forest Mall parking lot, and after that, the car was gone. We never had another.

Meanwhile, my dad—a lawyer—lived in a completely different world. He paid for child support and assumed that was enough. While I was boiling water on the stove for a bath at my mom's because we only had one tub and no hot water went to it, he told himself I was "taken care of."

That contrast became my first education in systemic gaps. I was living them. And when I entered college—first-generation, four jobs, no blueprint—I felt that weight. I had to claw my way into every room, and once I got there, I knew I didn't speak the same language.

But I never forgot the grind it took to get there. And that has made all the difference in how I lead today.

Intersectionality: Trauma Doesn't Live in a Vacuum

Socioeconomic trauma doesn't exist in isolation, it overlaps with race, gender, ability, and more. Kimberlé Crenshaw's concept of intersectionality gives us a lens to see that clearly.

A black woman living in poverty may experience racialized trauma layered with economic and gender-based stressors.

A disabled individual with financial means might still face medical trauma, isolation, and institutional bias.

An immigrant family working multiple jobs may be navigating cultural disconnection, language barriers, and the threat of deportation—all while trying to survive economically.

The more identities you carry, the more layered the trauma becomes. And yet, our systems still try to treat everyone as though they're starting from the same place.

How Chronic Stress Hijacks the Body

The nervous system isn't designed for ongoing threats. Poverty, food insecurity, housing instability—these are not "stressful events." They are entire environments of threat. When you grow up in survival mode, your baseline becomes dysregulation. Fight, flight, freeze—on a loop.

This is why trauma-informed care matters. Because traditional mental health frameworks often ignore the body, or the fact that it's still living inside the trauma. Therapies like EMDR help. They allow us to process the trauma without drowning in it again. But without access—without insurance, time off, or providers who understand—healing remains a luxury. And that's not okay.

From Survival to Systemic Insight

When you grow up poor, you learn how much of life performance is. I've walked into rooms where people judged me by my last name, my car, my shoes. Where "being articulate" shocked them. As if poverty and intelligence can't coexist.

But here's what those rooms never understood: Survival taught me more about strategy, empathy, and grit than any textbook ever could. I don't need to be invited to your table. I'm building one where people like me are already seated.

Rooted in Lived Experience

Being the first in my family to graduate from college (on my mom's side) wasn't just an academic achievement; it was an act of rebellion. I wasn't just earning a degree. I was tearing down a wall. That wall between "people like us" and "people like them."

I didn't stop at one degree. I got two master's. I built a private practice. I built a company. And now I lead from a place that honors the people who never made it to the table—not because they weren't worthy, but because the system was designed to keep them out.

I carry that with me in every leadership decision I make. It's not performative. It's personal.

Socioeconomics and the Spectrum of Trauma

1. Financial Stressors
Unpredictable income, eviction threats, food insecurity—these aren't abstract concerns. They are daily realities that keep nervous systems in overdrive.

2. Occupational Hazards
Low-income jobs are often the most physically dangerous and emotionally draining. No benefits. No sick days. No flexibility.

3. Health Inequities
Chronic illnesses, untreated trauma, and generational stress manifest as real physical conditions. Access to care can mean the difference between survival and collapse.

4. Isolation and Stigma
Communities with more resources often have more social support. Meanwhile, poverty isolates—both physically and emotionally. Shame thrives in silence.

Compassion Over Comparison

Trauma is not a competition. It doesn't matter if your pain came from a mansion or a shelter. What matters is how your body holds it. What matters is how your heart endured it. What matters is that we start listening to one another, instead of ranking our wounds.

Healing and the Bigger Picture

Healing is personal. But it's also political. When we understand the link between trauma and socioeconomic status, we stop blaming individuals for their struggles and start addressing the systems that created them.

This work is about more than therapy, it's about justice. It's about compassion. It's about unlearning what we've been taught about who deserves to be okay.

So, the next time you catch yourself judging someone's pain, ask: What don't I see? What might they be carrying that's invisible to me?

Final Reflections: We Heal Together

This chapter isn't just about me. It's about every person who's ever felt invisible, unworthy, or left behind because of where they come from. You are not broken, you are resourceful. You've survived things most people can't even imagine.

And you don't have to do it alone.

The truth is: healing is hard—but it becomes possible when we make space for each other's truths.

That's the real work. That's the revolution.

Chapter 10

THE LONELINESS OF BECOMING

Here's the thing about healing: It changes everything. And not just in the ways you expect.

Yes, it brings clarity. Yes, it brings alignment, peace, empowerment, and reconnection to self. But it also brings something harder to talk about: loss.

Because when you begin to heal—*really* heal—you start to see things you can't unsee. The friendships that only worked because you tolerated too much. The family dynamics that were built on silence, people-pleasing, or survival. The ways you used to shrink yourself just to be accepted.

And once you see it—once you *feel* the weight of how much you've been carrying—you can't go back.

This part of healing? It's lonely. Not because you're doing it wrong, but because you're doing it *honestly*.

There were seasons where I felt more disconnected than ever—not because I wasn't growing, but because I was. And growth often means outgrowing the roles you were once praised for. You stop over-functioning, and people call you selfish. You say "no," and they call you distant. You set boundaries, and suddenly you're "hard to reach."

But here's what I've learned:

Healing doesn't always bring connection. Sometimes it brings separation. Sometimes it's the bridge — and sometimes it's the border.

And that hurts. Because even if the old patterns weren't healthy, they were *familiar*. And walking away from what's familiar—even when it's toxic—is grief.

I wish we talked about this more. How healing can mean losing the very people you once broke yourself to belong to. How it can mean spending nights alone instead of pretending in a room full of people. How it can mean feeling like you don't quite fit *anywhere*—not the old life, not yet the new.

But here's what I can promise you: That space in between? It doesn't last forever. New connections come. Aligned friendships. Safer love. Relationships that don't require a mask.

But you must be willing to stand in the discomfort first— To hold the ache of what you lost, to receive the truth of who you're becoming.

This is the *real* sacred work. The part no one glamorizes. The part where you choose *you*—even when it costs you everything you thought you needed.

Embracing the Hidden Self: Shadow Work and Inner Child Healing

Shadow work and inner child healing are two of the most transformative tools in the trauma recovery toolkit. They allow us to unearth, understand, and integrate the wounded or suppressed aspects of ourselves—parts shaped by trauma, shame, neglect, or societal expectations. While this work is deeply uncomfortable at times, it offers something rare in the healing journey: the chance to reclaim wholeness.

Many people cringe when they first hear about "talking to your inner child." I get it—it can sound cliché or performative. But once I was truly engaged with this work, it cracked something open in me. These practices have helped me connect to parts of myself I didn't even know were still hurting—and gave me language to honor those wounds with compassion instead of judgment.

Shadow Work: Facing the Parts We Hide

Shadow work is about acknowledging the pieces of us we've learned to reject—the anger, jealousy, insecurity, or grief we were told were "too much," "inappropriate," or "unbecoming." As Carl Jung put it, "The shadow is the part of ourselves we don't want to be." But what we resist persists—and what we integrate becomes power.

Steps of Shadow Work:

1. Self-Reflection

Identify emotional triggers, repetitive relationship dynamics, or self-sabotaging behaviors. These are often clues pointing to unresolved pain or internalized beliefs.

Ask yourself: "What am I afraid people will see? Where do I overreact or shut down? What am I still carrying?"

2. Acknowledgment

Shadow work requires us to stop pretending. To stop saying "I'm fine" when we're not. It asks us to name our uncomfortable truths without shame or defensiveness—and to own them.

3. Uncovering Internalized Beliefs

Much of our shadow is inherited—formed by the narrative's others projected onto us.

Beliefs like: "I'm not enough," "I'm too much," or "I have to earn love" didn't come from nowhere. Unlearning these requires us to trace them back to their origin and consciously choose different truths.

4. Emotional Release

Whether through journaling, art, therapy, or movement—repressed emotions need a way out. Anger, fear, and grief that go unexpressed don't disappear. They fester. And over time, they shape how we see ourselves and the world.

5. Integration

The goal isn't to banish the shadow—it's to understand and integrate it. Only then can we move from fragmentation to wholeness. Integration looks like acceptance without self-betrayal. It's the ability to say, "This is a part of me—and I'm still worthy of love."

Inner Child Healing: Reconnecting to the Versions of You That Still Hurt

If shadow work is about the hidden self, inner child work is about the neglected one. The inner child holds our earliest emotions, unmet needs, and developmental wounds. These parts don't just disappear with age—they live in our nervous system and show up when we least expect it.

- When someone doesn't respond to a text, and you spiral into shame.
- When conflict makes you shut down or over-explain.
- When you feel unworthy in relationships, even when you're giving everything.

That's often not the adult; it's the inner child asking for safety.

Reconnecting with Your Inner Child:

- **Visualization:** Picture yourself at a younger age. What does that version of you need to hear?

- **Letter Writing:** Write to your younger self with compassion and validation.

- **Creating Safety:** Imagine a space where your inner child feels completely safe—then visit that space often in meditation or reflection.

Reparenting

Reparenting means becoming the caregiver you never had. It's setting boundaries. It's giving yourself permission to rest. It's speaking to yourself with gentleness instead of criticism. And it's recognizing that you are no longer powerless.

The Many Faces of the Inner Child

Inner child work isn't limited to your five-year-old self. Every trauma, betrayal, and rupture creates a new "inner version" of you that may have never fully processed the experience.

Lately, I've been doing work with my teenage self. She's fierce. She's hurt. She's got something to say—and I'm finally listening.

Healing her means making space for anger, for questioning, for the edges I was taught to stand down. It's exhausting. It's liberating. It's necessary.

The Rosebush

Growing up, there was a rosebush beside the garage. I remember picking roses, getting pricked, and running inside with my hands scratched and bleeding.

I keep thinking about that memory lately. It feels symbolic—this instinct I've always had to find beauty in places that hurt me. To keep reaching, even when it stings.

The Music That Raised Me

When I was a child, I ran to school in the winter just to sing Christmas songs in the auditorium before class started. Music was my sanctuary. Now I ask myself—why am I not chasing that same joy anymore? Why did I stop creating spaces where I could fully be myself?

Final Reflections: The Inner Work Is Ongoing—But Worth It

If you've ever wondered:
- Why do I keep dating the same kind of person?
- Why do I shrink around certain people?
- Why do I feel disconnected from myself?

Shadow work and inner child healing can answer those questions—not by fixing you, but by helping you remember who you were before you learned to hide.

Healing isn't about going back. It's about uncovering what was buried. It's about meeting the parts of you that were left behind—and bringing them home.

You're not broken.

You're rediscovering.

And the most important relationship you'll ever rebuild is the one with yourself.

Part Three

HEALING AS IDENTITY

Chapter 11

CALLED TO THE WORK: BECOMING A THERAPIST

I didn't become a therapist because I had it all figured out. I became a therapist because I *needed* to understand what I had lived through.

At first, the decision came from curiosity—that hunger to make sense of things no one had ever explained to me. The way people change. The way pain shapes us. The way trauma whispers into our choices, our relationships, our silence. But under that curiosity was something deeper—something that only now, in hindsight, I can name: I wanted to help others the way I once needed to be helped.

After I completed my first master's degree, I was working and excelling as an academic advisor. No one had ever told me how to be great at it—but it came naturally. And quickly, I realized I wasn't just helping students plan courses or avoid academic probation.

They weren't calling to drop a class. They were calling because they were overwhelmed. Because they didn't feel seen. Because life was hard and they didn't have a roadmap.

And that's what I gave them: strategies, tools, and compassion. I worked collaboratively with instructors and students. We *listened*. We *validated*. We created plans that considered the *whole person*—not just their Grade Point Average (GPA.)

That was my turning point.

I realized I was already doing therapeutic work—just without the formal title. So I made the decision to pursue a second master's degree. I wanted to do more than advise. I wanted to *hold space.* I wanted to be equipped to go deeper.

To me, being a therapist is more than a profession. It's a calling. It's a sacred space—one I don't take for granted.

A mentor once told me:

"It is an honor and a privilege to have people share their stories with you."

I have carried that wisdom with me every day since. Even in

the hard moments. Especially in the hard moments.

Because this work—the *real* work—is never about fixing. It's about witnessing. It's about presence. It's about creating space for people to find their own answers, at their own pace, in their own way.

This path helped me heal. It gave shape to my sensitivity. It turned my pain into purpose. And it keeps me grounded in the belief that healing is not only possible—it's *sacred*.

The Crown of Leadership—Navigating Trauma and Triumph

Leadership, like trauma, is an unrelenting paradox: It holds both pain and power, pressure and purpose. It demands self-awareness, adaptability, emotional regulation, and an unwavering commitment to integrity—even when everything inside you feels uncertain. For those with trauma histories, leadership doesn't just highlight our strengths. It also shines a glaring light on the wounds we thought we had already healed.

This section explores the intricate dance of leading while healing—how trauma shapes leadership styles, decision-making, interpersonal dynamics, and our sense of identity. It also invites the reader to reflect on the tension between internal healing and external responsibility. Because wearing the crown of leadership isn't just about directing others; it's about staying aligned with yourself, even when it's hard.

Leading Through a Trauma-Informed Lens

Emotional Resilience and the Cost of Survival

Trauma rewires our nervous systems. It teaches us to scan for danger, to prepare for abandonment, to anticipate failure—even when there's no evidence it's coming.

In leadership, these trauma responses can manifest as:
- Hyper-independence ("I'll just do it myself.")

- Over-control ("I can't trust anyone else to get it right.")
- Emotional numbing ("I don't have time to feel.")
- Chronic burnout masked as productivity

One of the hardest lessons I've learned is how to pause and ask: "Is this a trauma response or a leadership decision?" That single question has changed how I lead—and how I care for myself while doing it.

The Leadership Shadow

Every leader has a shadow. For some, it's ego. For others, it's imposter syndrome, perfectionism, or the constant drive to over-achieve. For trauma survivors, the shadow often whispers: "You're not enough." And so, we try to compensate—working harder, saying "yes" too often, sacrificing rest, and avoiding vulnerability.

Learning to use tools like *Wise Mind*—a dialectical behavior therapy (DBT) skill that balances emotion and logic—has helped me navigate those internal voices. It has also helped me lead with greater clarity, humility, and presence.

Real leadership isn't about performing competence. It's about being whole—even in the mess.

The Weight of Leadership

Leadership will test you. Not once. Repeatedly. You will be challenged by others. You will be challenged by systems. But most of all, you will be challenged by yourself.

For trauma survivors, every critique can feel like an attack. Every disagreement can register as betrayal. Every challenge can feel like confirmation that you were never meant to lead in the first place.

But not every hard moment is a threat. And not every reaction is reality. Sometimes it's just trauma showing up in disguise.

I've had to learn to differentiate between a challenge that requires courage—and a trigger that requires compassion.

When You're Expected to Be the Strong One

There's a myth that leaders are supposed to be unshakable. That strength means silence. That if you're struggling, you're weak—or worse, failing.

But real strength is being able to say, "I'm not okay today, and I'm still here." "I need support, not because I'm incapable, but because I'm human."

The truth is that many leaders are silently carrying unbearable emotional loads. The responsibility. The expectations. The fear that if you fall apart, the whole system might collapse with you.

Leadership shouldn't cost you your humanity. The crown is heavy.

Trauma-Informed Leadership in Action

Leadership, at its best, creates cultures of safety—not fear. It cultivates transparency, not secrecy. It encourages curiosity instead of shame.

Being trauma-informed as a leader means:
- Looking beyond behavior and asking, "What's really going on?"
- Creating environments where your team feels safe to speak up
- Regulating your own nervous system before responding to conflict

It also means understanding the difference between hypervigilance and awareness. Not every issue is sabotage. Not every conflict is rejection.

Trauma-informed leadership doesn't just serve your team. It changes the system from the inside out.

Ethics, Integrity, and Uncompromising Values

There have been many times I wished I could "just let it go." That I could be quieter, less passionate, easier to manage.

But I can't. Because I see what's broken in the mental health field—systems that profit off suffering, policies that uphold injustice, leadership models that reward performance over presence.

And every time I've tried to mute my voice, it felt like a betrayal of the very people I serve.

If you care deeply, you will be told you're too much. But if we don't fight for change, who will?

When Imposter Syndrome Creeps In

Here's what no one tells you about leadership: It doesn't matter how many degrees you earn, awards you win, or rooms you command—imposter syndrome still finds its way in.

- Who am I to lead?
- What if they find out I don't know what I'm doing?
- What if I fail?

Those thoughts don't mean you're unqualified. They mean you're human. And often, they mean your nervous system is trying to protect you from past experiences of rejection, exclusion, or failure.

Imposter syndrome and trauma drive often run side by side. But knowing the difference allows you to choose grounded action instead of reactive doubt.

The Calling Doesn't Go Away

There are days I fantasize about walking away from all of it. The stress. The expectations. The vulnerability of being seen.

But the calling doesn't stop. It knocks louder. It wakes me up at 2 a.m. It whispers: "You're not done yet."

Leadership isn't about being ready. It's about answering the call—even when you're scared. Especially when you're scared.

The Power of Showing Up

I once had four major presentations in one week. By the time I got to the fourth one, I was running on empty. My voice shook. My chest was tight. But I did it.

I spoke through the fear. I stood in my truth. And when I finished, the applause didn't matter as much as the knowing: *I showed up.* Not perfectly. But powerfully.

Perfectionism used to silence me. Now, I let the shaking voice speak anyway.

Confidence isn't the absence of fear. It's choosing to keep going in the presence of it.

Final Reflections: Leadership as a Sacred Responsibility

Leadership is not about control. It's about service. It's not about having all the answers. It's about listening deeply and acting with integrity. It's not about being perfect. It's about being present.

For those of us who lead from lived experience, this is the work:
- To create what we never had
- To advocate for what we once needed
- To stand in rooms where others told us we didn't belong

Leadership is a sacred responsibility. It's not light. It's not easy. But it is necessary. Especially now.

So, if you've been called to lead, even if your voice shakes, even if the crown feels heavy answer. Not because you're unafraid. But because you've already survived more than most will ever know.

You were made for this.

Chapter 12

THE MOMENT I ALMOST WALKED AWAY

If you haven't figured it out yet—when I decide, I stand ten toes down on it. I don't waver. I don't stall. I move.

And after my brother died, I made a decision. I was done.

I went to bed one night fully committed to walking away from being a therapist and not publishing my first book. I had told myself: "This is it. I can't hold space for others when I'm breaking inside. I'll start telling my patients tomorrow."

I wasn't angry at the profession. I just couldn't imagine continuing when the weight of my own grief felt unbearable. How could I keep guiding others when I couldn't even save one of the people who mattered most to me?

So, I went to bed with that decision pressed into my chest. And then . . . I had a dream.

In the dream, I was standing before a massive, swirling galaxy of stars—vast, brilliant, silent. It didn't say anything, but I remember thinking, "God? Is that you?" And then, through the center of the galaxy, two enormous white wings emerged—soft, radiant, powerful.

I didn't know what else to do, so I reached toward the wings. And I asked: "What am I supposed to do?"

And a voice—calm, clear, undeniable—replied: "You know what to do."

I jolted awake. Heart racing. Mind spinning. And my very first thought was: "Is God Dumbledore? Because that was the most cryptic riddle I've ever received."

But once the humor settled, the meaning hit me: I *did* know what to do. Strap on the wings. Keep going. Don't quit.

That dream pulled me back from the edge. It reminded me that this work—my work—is bigger than me. That my brother's memory *needed* to live through the words I hadn't yet written. That the people sitting across from me—the ones who were holding on by a thread—still needed a place to fall apart and be held.

So, I stayed. I kept my practice open. I published my first book. I honored the pain—and I kept showing up anyway.

Not because it was easy. But because it was sacred. And because deep down, I knew: This is what I was made for.

Trauma & Protection—Navigating Safety and Healing

Trauma and protection are intricately bound—two forces in constant conversation. Trauma disrupts our sense of safety, trust, and control, while protection becomes the armor we craft in response. For many survivors, protection is not a luxury, it's a lifeline. But as healing begins, that armor can become a barrier to connection, vulnerability, and growth.

In this chapter, we examine the nervous system's role in protection, how trauma shapes our sense of safety, and the fine line between empowered boundaries and self-isolating defenses. Healing is not just about feeling safe, it's about learning we are *worthy* of safety in the first place.

1. When Safety Is Stripped Away

The most immediate casualty of trauma is safety.

When trauma enters our lives:
- Our nervous systems shift into survival—fight, flight, freeze, fawn, or flop.
- Trust evaporates, even in previously "safe" relationships.
- Hypervigilance becomes our baseline—always scanning, bracing, waiting.

For many survivors, safety feels theoretical—something others might have access to, but never us. It becomes easier to rely on control, isolation, or numbness than to risk being open again.

2. Protection as a Survival Strategy

After trauma, we learn to protect ourselves in any way we can.

Emotionally:
- Avoidance, people-pleasing, detachment, over-explaining, or shutting down

Physically:
- Weight gain or loss, muscle armor, disordered eating, posture changes

Relationally:
- Hyper-independence, pushing others away, trauma bonding, choosing chaos over absence

These are not flaws. They're adaptations. But when survival mode becomes our default, protection may keep us alive—while also keeping us disconnected.

3. The DBT House Exercise

In one of my graduate programs, we did a Dialectical Behavior Therapy (DBT) exercise where we were asked to build a symbolic "house." The question was: who or what protects the roof of your house?

My roof held only one name—mine.

Everyone else listed loved ones, mentors, or spiritual beliefs. My house stood alone, protected only by me. That image stayed with me. It reminded me just how deeply I had internalized the belief that *I am the only one who will ever protect me.*

I've mistaken intimacy for safety and relationships for rescue, only to be reminded—over and over—that my self-protection runs deeper than my desire for connection.

And the more I reinforce the roof, the harder it is to let anyone in.

4. The Isolation of Protection

Sometimes what we call "boundaries" are just walls. Sometimes we say, "I'm independent," when what we mean is "I don't trust anyone to show up."

I want connection. I crave safety. But I've spent so long armoring myself that even tenderness feels like a threat.

This is the paradox:
We want to be held, but we flinch at being touched.
We want to be seen, but we hide in plain sight.
We want protection, but not at the cost of our autonomy.

And somewhere in that tug-of-war, we begin to ask: "Am I isolating out of choice, or out of fear?"

5. The Nervous System Doesn't Lie

The belief that "I am not safe" isn't just a thought—it's a bodily state.

The body holds trauma:
- Tense shoulders
- Clenched jaw
- Shallow breath
- Constant alertness, even during rest or joy

I tell my clients, "Trust your body," but what happens when the body only knows defense? What happens when even peace feels unfamiliar?

Learning to *feel* safe is one of the most difficult and transformative parts of healing.

6. When Weight Becomes Protection

Weight has been both a shield and a protest.

At different points in my life, my body has expanded not just from biology or habits, but from a desire to be unseen, unsexualized, or underestimated. Sometimes my body armor was subconscious. Other times, it was a conscious rejection of systems that told me I had to shrink to be worthy.

People talk about bodies as if they're public property—com-

menting on size, weight, shape, and tone. It's not just intrusive.
It's unnecessary.

Comments like:
  • "You're confident for your size."
  • "You looked so good back then."
  • "You carry your weight well."

Every remark serves as a reminder: For many, worth is still measured in pounds, not presence. But I am not here to be palatable.
I am here to be *whole*.

7. The Fantasy of Protection

For a long time, I believed that love would keep me safe. That someone could step in, wrap me in warmth, and make the past irrelevant.
    But love that is controlling is not protection. Love that requires shrinking is not safety. Love that silences your intuition is not healing.
    I mistook attachment for belonging. I believed that if I just held on tightly enough, I wouldn't be abandoned. But instead, I ended up alone—once again—fortifying my own roof.

8. The Journey Back to Safety

Healing is realizing:
  • Safety is not found in isolation or dependence.
  • Safety is not guaranteed in love or relationship.
  • Safety is built through regulation, boundaries, and self-trust.
  • True safety is in your ability to stay with yourself.
  • To sit in stillness and not run.
  • To trust your body and your voice.
  • To feel fear and choose presence anyway.

Safety becomes real the moment you stop outsourcing it.

Final Reflections: Reclaiming Protection as Power

I used to believe safety was something other people had—something I was denied because of what I'd been through. But I was wrong. Safety is a birthright. It's not something you wait to receive. It's something you learn to cultivate.

"No one is coming to save me" once felt like devastation. Now, it feels like a reclamation.

I protect myself today—not because I expect betrayal, but because I value peace. I build safety not through control or isolation, but through trusting myself, in the process, in the people who earn it.

Healing means we no longer confuse protection with fear. We choose it from love.

Chapter 13

THE WINGS I WEAR NOW

I didn't ask for the wings. I didn't go looking for them. They came to me—in the middle of grief, doubt, and surrender—when I was ready to walk away from everything I had built.

They weren't a promise of ease. They were a reminder of purpose.

One of the tools that helped me—and still helps me—is my spirituality. Not the kind found in a rulebook or ritual, but the kind that speaks in dreams and symbols, silence and stars. That dream wasn't just random. It was *guidance*. It was *proof* that I wasn't alone in this work. That something bigger was holding me, calling me, reminding me: *You are still needed. You are still meant for this.*

Spirituality became a lifeline—not because it gave me answers, but because it gave me *connection*. To the unseen. To the sacred. To my brother. To a deeper truth I could trust, even when nothing else made sense.

I used to think healing would feel like peace. Now I know it also feels like *weight*. Like responsibility. Like showing up even when it's hard. Like staying, when you want to run.

These wings aren't made of light. They're made of every story I've held. Every client I've walked with. Every trauma I've survived. Every truth I've finally spoken. And yes—they are also made of him. My brother. The ache and the love and the lessons I carry with me, every day I keep going.

So now, when I question the path ... when I feel the doubt creeping in again ... I remember the voice: *You know what to do.*

And I do. I strap on the wings. And I keep going.

Preach Vulnerability

Preach vulnerability—to others
Embrace vulnerability—with others
Bathe in vulnerability—among others
Now it's your turn.
Can you actually do what you've preached?
Can you practice what you've claimed to believe?
Can you allow others to truly see you?

Going Within: A Double-Edged Sword

"Going within" sounds peaceful—like a meditative retreat where answers unfold in stillness. But what if your internal world isn't calm? What if you're "within" is a battlefield scarred by years of survival?

For me, disconnection from my body wasn't just a coping mechanism—it was survival. My body was not mine for a long time. It had been shaped, used, and misrepresented by trauma and the stories others wrote about me.

Reconnection meant reopening wounds I thought I had buried. It meant confronting the abuse I tolerated, the pain I couldn't control, and the long stretches of time I spent dissociating just to endure. Avoidance felt safer. Detachment was comforting. But deep down, I knew the longer I avoided the pain, the louder it would scream.

And it did.

It showed up in panic attacks, chronic tension, emotional outbursts, and a persistent feeling of being ungrounded—like I didn't truly belong in my own skin. Survival mode had been my baseline for so long, I couldn't imagine life beyond it.

Stuck in the Mud: The Temptation to Stay

It's tempting to stay stuck. The mud may be cold, messy, and limiting—but at least it's familiar. Growth sounds noble, but it threatens the identity trauma that has helped you build. When trauma becomes your anchor, healing can feel like betrayal.

So, let's be clear: What happened to you was not your fault. How you heal is your choice. And it's okay if that choice feels hard.

Your story is yours. You get to decide how it unfolds from here.

I remember one of my lowest moments. My sister asked, "How do you want to be remembered, Kaitlyn?"

I laughed it off with sarcasm. But that question stuck with me. It echoed in my mind. If I kept going the way I was—numbing out, avoiding healing, I knew exactly how I'd be remembered: as someone who didn't make it. As someone whose pain swallowed them whole.

But I had always carried a quiet "knowing"—that I was meant for something more. That I could change the narrative.

I remember saying to myself: "I want to be remembered as someone who gave a damn."

Relatable Reflections: Growing Through Trauma

1. Recognizing Triggers

I once walked into a room and heard a song my brother used to love. Suddenly, I wasn't in the present—I was in grief's grip. Triggers like that are time machines. But now, I meet them with grounding techniques, like breathwork or quietly stepping away. Triggers don't mean I'm broken. They mean I'm still connected to something that mattered.

2. Avoidance Patterns

For a long time, I avoided certain places because of what they reminded me of. Driving past one particular building would send me spiraling. Avoidance made me feel safe—for a while. But it also kept me frozen. Eventually, I learned to let those memories exist without letting them control me.

3. Building Resilience

One of my clients once said, "I don't think I'm strong enough." I replied, "You already are. You survived it." That moment taught me something about myself, too. Each time I chose to confront my pain instead of running, I proved I could grow. I wasn't just surviving, I was evolving.

4. Setting Boundaries

Saying "no" was once unthinkable for me. I had spent so long people-pleasing, overextending, and betraying myself for others' comfort. But each boundary I set was a small act of liberation. Healing meant reclaiming my time, energy, and peace.

5. Practicing Self-Compassion

I used to berate myself for every misstep. I thought self-criticism was accountability. Now, I talk to myself like I would like a friend. When I fall short, I remind myself: "You're doing your best." Self-compassion is a muscle—and it's saved me more than once.

The Version of Me I Miss

Sometimes I miss the version of me that didn't care. The one who was reckless, impulsive, unapologetically raw. But she was also hurting. She was surviving with no roadmap, no lifeline. And she made choices that carried lasting consequences.

I don't have to grieve her entirely. I can honor her courage and defiance while letting go of her chaos. I don't miss her suffering—but I do admire her fire.

I tell my patients, "I have body bags full of mistakes." I'm no longer defined by them, and they don't weigh what they once did—but they still exist. Healing hasn't erased my past. It's just made it easier to carry.

Knowing Yourself to Process Trauma

Knowing yourself isn't a destination, it's an ongoing practice. Healing requires curiosity about your inner world: your reactions, your stories, your patterns.

Here's what I've learned:

- **Triggers are Teachers.** They show you where you're still hurting and offer insight into what needs attention.

- **Boundaries are Freedom.** They're not walls. They're ways of choosing yourself with intention.

- **Self-Compassion is Survival.** Kindness isn't indulgent. It's how you stay grounded in a storm.

- **Healing is Nonlinear.** Some days you'll soar. Other days you'll sink. Both are part of the journey.

How Do You Want to Be Remembered?

That question from my sister made a profound impact. I had been living in reaction, in defense, in collapse. But legacy is not born out of survival's born from intention.

Healing doesn't erase the past. It gives you the power to write what comes next.

Your trauma is not your identity. It's a chapter, not your whole story.

So, ask yourself: "How do I want to be remembered?" And let that answer shape what you choose next.

Chapter 14
UNMASKING THE DIAGNOSIS

For most of my life, I didn't have the language to describe what I was experiencing. I just thought I was "too much"—too sensitive, too intense, too complicated. I felt like I was always trying to decode a world that everyone else seemed to understand effortlessly. And when I couldn't, I blamed myself. So I worked harder. Masked better. Trying to be what everyone needs. And I got good at it.

But good masking comes at a cost—especially when you don't know you're doing it.

I thought all my exhaustion, social burnout, sensory overwhelm, and deep need for structure were byproducts of trauma. And while trauma was absolutely part of my story, it wasn't the *whole* story. There was something deeper. Something neurological. Something innate.

And finally, in adulthood, I had a word for it: *autistic.*

Getting that diagnosis—or for me, that deep, inner *knowing*—was like finally being handed the map I'd been looking for my whole life. It didn't solve everything, but it connected the dots. It gave context to the patterns I'd been living and fighting for decades.

It helped me stop asking, "What's wrong with me?" And start asking, "What do I *need* in order to feel safe, whole, and regulated?"

It made sense why I masked it so well—because I had to. Not just to avoid abandonment, but to function in a world that demanded I pretend to be neurotypical just to get by. But it also showed me that masking wasn't just about trauma—it was about survival in a society that doesn't understand neurodivergent wiring.

This realization was both liberating and devastating. Liberating, because it gave me a framework for compassion. Devastating, because I grieved the years I spent trying to "fix" myself instead of understanding myself.

Now, I no longer strive to be palatable. I strive to be regulated. To be aligned. To be true to the rhythm of *my* nervous system—

even if it doesn't look like anyone else's.

And that's what this chapter — and this *book* — is about: Unlearning the performance. Remembering the truth. And giving ourselves permission to exist as we are.

Unmasking the Truth—The Journey of Late-Diagnosed Autistic Women

For most of my life, I wore a mask I didn't know existed. It wasn't something I consciously created—it formed out of necessity. I learned to adapt, to perform, to survive. But it wasn't until writing this book, reflecting on trauma, and revisiting parts of myself that I had long silenced, that I began to see what had always been hidden in plain sight: I am autistic.

Not in the stereotypical or clinical way the world tends to recognize, but in the deeply personal, embodied experience of being a sensitive, intuitive, trauma-shaped woman who learned to mask her true self to navigate a neurotypical world.

This realization didn't arrive in a single epiphany—it was a slow unraveling. Each chapter I wrote, each memory I revisited, brought me closer to a truth I could no longer ignore. I wasn't just responding to trauma. I was also responding to a world that never fit.

Masking: The Art of Hiding in Plain Sight

Masking is a survival strategy many autistic individuals—especially women—use to blend into a society that was never designed for them. It's an invisible labor, often mistaken for social competence. But masking isn't harmless; it's exhausting. It's self-abandonment.

I had been doing it for as long as I could remember:
- Rehearsing conversations before speaking, then overanalyzing them afterward
- Mimicking others' body language and tone to avoid standing out

- Forcing eye contact, even when it felt invasive or over-whelming
- Suppressing stimming behaviors like tapping my fingers or bouncing my leg
- Constantly second-guessing myself: "Did I talk too much? Was I awkward? Did I say the wrong thing?"

At the time, I didn't know I was masking. I thought I was just being "good," "professional," "normal." I didn't realize I was hiding.

The Cost of Masking

Masking doesn't come without consequences. It drains your mental, emotional, and physical energy. It creates confusion around who you are. It disconnects you from your instincts and your identity.

For me, it looked like:
- Chronic emotional exhaustion after social interactions
- Deep confusion about why I felt so different, even in familiar spaces
- Years of misdiagnoses—anxiety, depression, ADHD, trauma—everything except the one thing that actually made sense
- A lingering sense of not belonging, even in rooms where I was loved or respected

The breaking point came when I finally admitted to myself that I wasn't *just* anxious. I wasn't *just* burned out. Something deeper was at play.

The Diagnosis Journey

I began researching late-diagnosed autistic women and immedi-ately saw myself reflected in their stories:

- Sensory sensitivities: bright lights, loud noises, irritating fabrics
- Deep, focused interests that bordered on obsession
- A strong need for routine and structure
- Recurrent burnout that left me feeling emotionally and physically depleted

For years, I resisted the idea. I told myself it didn't "fit." I worried it would be seen as another label or excuse. But eventually, I asked myself what I would tell a patient in my care—and the answer was clear: *Explore it. Without shame.*

So, I did.

In the fall of 2024, I scheduled my intake. The full testing process began in early 2025. It was comprehensive, rigorous, and more emotional than I expected. After multiple assessments and evaluations, I received my diagnosis: Autism Level 1 without intellectual impairment, alongside Generalized Anxiety Disorder.

Grieving the Girl Who Never Knew

I didn't feel relief. I didn't feel validation. I felt grief.

Grief for the girl who spent her childhood feeling wrong instead of different. Grief for the young woman who internalized shame instead of asking for support. Grief for the adult who built her life around masking instead of belonging.

The diagnosis didn't change who I was. It gave me language for what had always been there. It gave me a mirror I didn't know I needed.

I wasn't broken. I was misunderstood.

Why Women Are Diagnosed Late

Autistic women are chronically underdiagnosed for several reasons:

1. Diagnostic criteria were developed based on studies of young boys.

2. Women are typically more adept at social masking and cam-
   ouflage.

3. Autism in women often looks like something else—anxiety,
   depression, bipolar disorder (BPD), ADHD.

4. Many women are dismissed as being "too sensitive," "dramatic," or "difficult."

As a result, many of us go decades without knowing the truth. We
adapt to the world by erasing parts of ourselves. We pass as neurotypical while slowly unraveling inside.

The Process of Unmasking

Unmasking is not a one-time act—it's a lifelong process. It's not
about "becoming autistic." It's about reclaiming the self I had
buried beneath years of performance and perfectionism.

I began unmasking by:
- Allowing myself to stim freely without shame
- Speaking my truth, even when it made others uncomfortable
- Reassessing relationships based on who truly sees and
  accepts me
- Prioritizing environments that accommodate my sensory
  needs

Unmasking meant learning to exist without apology. It meant
allowing myself to take up space in a world that once told me I
was "too much."

The Intersection of Autism, Trauma, and Mental Health

Many late-diagnosed autistic women share a common thread:
trauma. Why?

Because we are often misdiagnosed, invalidated, and unprotected. Because we spend years ignoring our needs to survive. Because masking itself is a trauma—a form of prolonged self-erasure.

This book began as a trauma narrative. It evolved into an identity narrative. The two are inseparable. My trauma shaped how I masked. And my masking delayed my healing.

What Comes Next

I don't have all the answers. I don't know what unmasking will look like a year from now, or how this identity will continue to unfold. But I know this:

I am autistic.

I am unmasking.

I am still learning how to show up fully as myself.

This chapter isn't just about me—it's about every woman who has spent her life contorting, blending, masking, adapting. It's for the ones who were told they were "too intense," "too sensitive," "too much."

You are not too much. You are coming home to yourself. And that is everything.

Chapter 15

THROUGH A DIFFERENT LENS: NEURODIVERGENCE AND TRAUMA

For a long time, I didn't know I was neurodivergent. I just knew I felt *different and out of place.*

I processed things more deeply. I needed more structure, more recovery time, more space. I noticed things others didn't—the flicker of a light, the tension in a room, the shift in someone's tone. And while those things made me intuitive, they also made me exhausted.

Before I had the language of autism, I had a lifetime of feeling like I was "too much" or "not enough"—depending on the day. And layered over that was trauma. So much trauma.

Being neurodivergent shaped *how* I experienced trauma—and how deeply it impacted me.

- I didn't just *hear* painful words—I internalized them.
- I didn't just *feel* rejection—I *absorbed* it.
- I didn't just get overwhelmed—I became dysregulated in ways I couldn't explain.

The world already felt loud, fast, unpredictable. Add trauma to that—and the volume turned all the way up.

My masking didn't just come from trauma—it came from neurodivergence, too. It was a survival strategy I learned young: "If I can just be likable... if I can mirror people, blend in, shut down my needs... maybe I'll be safe. Maybe I'll belong."

But masking long-term, especially as a neurodivergent person, doesn't just hide who you are — it *fractures* you. It disconnects you from your body, your intuition, your sense of self. And for me, it made healing harder—because I didn't even know who the *real me* was.

Realizing I'm autistic was a massive unmasking moment. It reframed everything: The anxiety, the burnout, the overwhelm, the deep empathy, the rigidity, the sensory struggles—none of it was "wrong." It was just *me*—unaccommodated, misunderstood, and trying to survive in a world that wasn't designed with me in mind.

That realization didn't erase the trauma. But it helped me *understand* it. It gave context. It gave compassion. And it gave me permission to stop performing.

Now, I see my neurodivergence not as something to fix—but as something to *support*. I build my life around what works for my brain and body. I honor my needs unapologetically. And I hold space for others through a lens that's wider, deeper, and more attuned.

Because being neurodivergent didn't just affect my trauma—It also shaped how I *heal*.

Neurodivergence and Trauma: The Hidden Intersection

Looking back, it's clear now that my neurodivergence didn't just *exist* alongside my trauma—it *amplified* it.

Because I processed the world so deeply—every word, tone, silence, shift in energy—the wounds cut sharper. What might've rolled off someone else's back stayed with me like a scar under the skin. My nervous system was already hyperaware. Add trauma to that—and it was like living in a body that was always bracing for impact.

Here's how they tied together:

Abandonment:
Being autistic made it harder to navigate social dynamics, especially the unspoken ones. I often felt on the outside without knowing *why*. So, when someone pulled away—a friend, a partner, a family member—it didn't feel like a moment. It felt like *proof* that I was unlovable. Trauma turned that sensitivity into a core wound.

Sexual assault:
My sensory sensitivity meant that what happened didn't just violate my physical boundaries—it overloaded my entire system. I froze. I dissociated. And afterward, I couldn't find the words.

The overwhelm wasn't just emotional. It was neurological. And the shame ran deep—not just for what happened, but for how "strange" I felt in how I processed it.

Masking as survival:
I was already masking my neurodivergence just to function in a neurotypical world. Trauma added another mask: the one that said, "I'm fine." So I layered them—pretending to be okay when I wasn't, pretending to be "normal" when I was unraveling. And that double-masking nearly erased me.

Grief and loss:
When my brother died, I didn't just grieve—I unraveled. My brain doesn't compartmentalize easily. There are no neat boxes. Every memory, every feeling, every question flooded me at once. And without the right tools, I spiraled—into numbness, chaos, and a deep sense of isolation no one could see from the outside.

Understanding my neurodivergence has helped me make sense of why some traumas hit harder, lingered longer, and healed slower. It also gave me the ability to forgive myself for how I coped. For why I spiraled. For why I disconnected. For why I *survived the way I did.*

Because my brain wasn't broken. It was doing the best it could in a world that didn't understand it—during moments that almost broke it.

What I Thought Was Wrong with Me (But Was Really Autism)

- "Too sensitive" → Deep sensory processing
- "Too intense" → Hyper-empathy and emotional attunement
- "Bad at relationships" → Social burnout and communication mismatch
- "Always overwhelmed" → Chronic dysregulation, not weakness
- "Cold or detached" → Dissociation as protection
- "Can't let things go" → Pattern recognition and trauma looping

Unveiling the Mask—Navigating Trauma and Self-Protection

Masking, in the context of trauma, is more than a behavioral adaptation; it's a survival response. It's the way many of us learned to stay safe in environments that were anything but. For trauma survivors, masking becomes second nature: a way to fit in, to keep others comfortable, to hide pain so deeply we've forgotten what it feels like to live without it.

But unmasking? That's not as simple as "just be yourself." When survival has required hiding who you are, stepping into authenticity can feel like a risk. Because, at one point, it was.

This section explores the origins, purpose, and cost of masking—and the profound courage required to take it off.

Why We Mask

1. Protection from Further Harm

Many survivors adopt personas that help them avoid attention, confrontation, or vulnerability. For instance, a survivor of childhood abuse might develop a confident, no-nonsense exterior to signal strength and deflect perceived threats.

2. Coping with Shame and Stigma

To avoid judgment or pity, survivors often adopt roles: the strong one, the funny one, the achiever. Pain becomes a private burden, hidden beneath a polished surface.

3. Maintaining Control

When emotional expression was punished or used against us, suppressing feelings can feel like the only safe option. For some, appearing stoic becomes a shield against the chaos of inner emotional storms.

4. Preserving Relationships

Many survivors become people-pleasers in order to keep the peace. They say "yes" when they mean "no," swallow discomfort, and mirror others to maintain connection—even if it means losing themselves.

5. Surviving in Unsafe Environments

In toxic households, harmful partnerships, or oppressive workplaces, masking becomes essential. Some neurodivergent individuals, for example, learn to mimic neurotypical behaviors to avoid ridicule, discrimination, or exclusion.

6. Disconnection from the Self

The longer we mask, the further we drift from our authentic selves. Identity becomes fragmented. We forget what we like, what we need, and who we are beneath the performance.

7. Mental and Physical Exhaustion

Wearing a mask takes an enormous toll. It can lead to chronic fatigue, anxiety, depression, and emotional numbness. Eventually, something gives—the mask slips, or we break under the weight of holding it up.

The Two Sides of Masking

Masking works. It gets praise, promotions, and proximity. But it comes at a cost:
- We lose touch with our needs, desires, and identity.
- We miss out on genuine connection because we're never truly seen.
- We become emotionally and physically exhausted trying to maintain the facade.
- We internalize the belief that our true self is not acceptable, lovable, or safe.

Taking off the mask means confronting what we've buried—pain, grief, fear, unmet needs—and learning how to show up anyway.

Masking Through a Trauma Lens

Masking is not about deception. It's about safety.

From a trauma perspective, masking is an unconscious strategy to protect ourselves when no one else did. When we've experienced betrayal, neglect, or emotional invalidation, we develop behaviors to stay invisible or palatable.

We:
- Smile when we want to scream
- Make ourselves small to avoid retaliation
- Over-function to avoid criticism
- Disappear into roles that make others comfortable

I often tell my clients: *You didn't choose the mask—you adapted to survive. The mask was your protection when no one else showed up to protect you.*

But what once protected us eventually imprisons us. We forget how to take the mask off. Or worse—we're not sure who we are without it.

The Tragedy and the Truth

The world rewards masking. It applauds composure, resilience, and productivity—even when they're fueled by trauma. People see the results but not the cost.

The tragedy is that masking often works so well that even we start to forget what's underneath. The truth is that masking is often trauma itself: a slow, daily erasure of our own voice, needs, and nervous system cues.

We become masters of mimicry and silence. We learn how to be what others need while forgetting to ask what *we* need.

And the truth is this:
- We become overly agreeable to avoid conflict.
- We silence our needs to maintain connection.
- We stay busy so we won't have to feel.

- We laugh when we want to cry, and cry when no one's watching.

The Act of Unmasking

Unmasking is not just about taking something off—it's about coming back to yourself.

It's not easy. It requires you to feel the things you've numbed, to ask for what you've always denied yourself, to risk rejection for the sake of authenticity. But it's also the gateway to freedom.

Unmasking means:
- Saying, "No more pretending"
- Reclaiming your voice, your needs, your nervous system
- Choosing to stop betraying yourself to make others more comfortable

It is a declaration: *I am worthy of existing as I am. I am no longer willing to earn love through silence or sacrifice.*

Chapter 16

MASKING WASN'T THE TRAUMA— IT WAS THE RESPONSE TO BEING MISUNDERSTOOD

Let me be clear: My neurodivergence wasn't caused by trauma. And trauma didn't make me autistic.

I've always been this way—deeply sensitive, observant, intuitive, intense. I experienced the world differently, and that difference is something *I was born with.*

But *not knowing* I was neurodivergent? That shaped almost everything.

It meant that I spent years—decades—thinking there was something wrong with me. I couldn't keep up socially. I needed more rest than others. I got overstimulated easily. And the world didn't explain those experiences to me—it punished me for them. So I adapted.

I studied people. I mimicked behavior. I forced eye contact. I laughed on cue. I built a mask—not because I wanted to be fake, but because I wanted to be safe.

The trauma came in when that mask was the only version of me people accepted. When my needs were ignored, minimized, or punished. When I experienced abandonment, invalidation, and assault in a body and brain that already felt different and unseen. Being neurodivergent didn't *cause* the trauma—but it shaped how I experienced it. And not knowing I was autistic? That made me internalize every trauma as *my fault.*

Now I can separate the two: Trauma was something that *happened to me.* Neurodivergence is something that has *always been part of me.*

And understanding that has been one of the most freeing, healing realizations of my life.

It's allowed me to grieve what I didn't know. It's allowed me to reclaim the parts of myself I once masked. And it's allowed me to build a life that finally fits the way my mind and heart are wired.

Understanding the Landscape of Healing

Mental health is the foundation upon which every other aspect of our lives is built. It shapes how we process the world, relate to others, and experience ourselves. For those of us who carry trauma, mental health is often misunderstood—not because it lacks importance, but because it was never modeled as something to nurture, only something to push through or hide.

This section is a trauma-informed exploration of what mental health means, how it shows up in daily life, and why healing begins when we stop performing and start listening—to our bodies, our emotions, and our pain.

1. Core Components of Mental Health

Emotional Well-Being
- Recognizing and naming emotions without judgment
- Regulating emotions with tools like mindfulness, grounding, and therapy
- Giving yourself permission to feel, without apology

Psychological Well-Being
- Cultivating resilience—the capacity to recover from emotional wounds
- Developing cognitive awareness, recognizing distorted thinking patterns and reframing them
- Creating a mindset where progress matters more than perfection

Social Well-Being
- Maintaining authentic relationships that nourish, not drain
- Building a community where you feel seen, safe, and supported
- Letting go of connections rooted in performance or self-abandonment

Coping and Stress Management
- Learning to self-regulate instead of self-destruct
- Replacing old patterns (like overworking, isolating, or numbing) with adaptive tools
- Practicing distress tolerance skills and nervous system regulation

Daily Functioning
- Engaging in activities that bring purpose, not just productivity
- Allowing rest and joy to coexist with ambition and responsibility
- Asking yourself not just "What do I need to do?" but also "What do I need to feel okay?"

2. The Mental Health Continuum

Mental health is not static. It lives on a continuum, shifting day to day—or moment to moment. You can function well and still struggle. You can feel joy and still grieve. That's not failure; that's humanity.

- Mental health challenges may include:
- Anxiety and panic disorders
- Mood disorders like depression or BPD
- Trauma-related disorders such as PTSD or complex PTSD
- Neurodivergence: ADHD, Autism, sensory processing challenges

These diagnoses are not character flaws. They're responses—often to stress, trauma, environment, or biology. The goal isn't to label; the goal is to understand what's happening and to offer care and support accordingly.

3. My Mental Health Journey—The Wake-Up Call

I didn't become a clinician because I always knew I would. I became one because I couldn't ignore what was right in front of me. As an academic advisor, I noticed that students weren't failing because of poor time management. They were drowning in anxiety, grief, often undiagnosed symptoms. No one had taught them how to cope—so I did.

And then I started paying attention to my own mental health:
- I assumed my anxiety was just "being responsible."
- I thought depressive episodes were laziness or burnout.
- I blamed myself for being "too much" rather than considering neurodivergence.

Eventually, I had to face the truth: I wasn't just surviving; I was running on fumes. And it was starting to catch up with me.

4. The Trauma Drive—When Burnout Looks Like Success

One of the most insidious parts of trauma is the way it drives overachievement. We become addicted to productivity, praise, and performance because they mask emptiness inside.

I wasn't thriving. I was compensating.
- I worked late because resting felt unsafe.
- I over-functioned because it distracted me from my grief.
- I succeeded because failure would've confirmed my worst fears about myself.

But the trauma drive will burn you out. And eventually, your body will force you to stop.

5. Healing Beyond the Diagnosis

As a clinician, I've learned not to treat diagnoses as gospel. They can be helpful and provide a framework or context, but they don't always tell the full story.

Here's what really matters:
- Do your symptoms interfere with your daily life?
- Are you able to manage stress without shutting down or lashing out?
- Do you feel safe in your body—or like you're constantly bracing for impact?

Healing means working with what's present—not waiting for a label to give you permission to start.

6. Anxiety: The Nervous System on High Alert

Anxiety is not "just worrying." It's a full-body experience—one that roots itself in both mind and muscle.

Cognitive symptoms:
- Racing thoughts, catastrophizing, obsessive rumination
- Inability to turn off the "what ifs"

Physical symptoms:
- Digestive issues, headaches, fatigue
- Muscle tension, chest tightness, difficulty breathing

Behavioral symptoms:
- Avoidance, people-pleasing, hyper-productivity
- Over-apologizing, reassurance-seeking, withdrawing

Anxiety isn't weakness—it's your body trying to protect you. But when the alarm never turns off, it becomes a prison.

Trauma and Addiction—The Search for Nothingness

There was a time in my life when I chased numbness. Not joy, not connection—just the absence of pain. And substances made that possible. Whether it was drugs and alcohol (back in the day), or workaholism, I was just trying to escape myself.

I hit a turning point the night I watched someone I loved nearly die in front of me—while everyone else stood frozen. That moment cracked something open in me. It didn't change everything overnight, but it forced me to reckon with the truth: I was heading down a path I wouldn't return from.

After my brother died, I picked up alcohol again—only to find that it no longer worked. My body was rejecting what my mind still craved. That's when I realized: it wasn't the substance I missed. It was the illusion of peace. The mask.

Replacing Addiction with Achievement

When I gave up on substances in my early twenties, I didn't magically get better—I just found a more socially acceptable addiction: success. I traded one high for another. Overworking. Over giving. Overachieving. It looked like healing. But it wasn't.

That's the trap. We think we've healed because we've "moved on"—but really, we've just reshaped the dysfunction. Trauma doesn't disappear because you got a new job or reached a goal. It disappears when you stop needing the high or numbness to feel okay.

Mental Health is Not a Destination

Healing is not linear. It's not a single transformation—it's a series of thousands. You will backslide. You will question everything. You will feel like you're starting over more times than you can count.

But each time, you'll come back stronger. More self-aware. More whole.

You are allowed to rest. You are allowed to feel. You are allowed to take up space without performing wellness for the sake of others.

Mental health isn't about being happy all the time—it's about being honest with where you are and compassionate with yourself when you get there.

Final Reflections: If You're Going Through Hell, Keep Going

Sometimes, I still feel lost. But I've learned that feeling lost doesn't mean you've failed, it means you're still searching. Still moving. Still alive.

And when the trauma drive starts whispering again, I remind myself: I'm not here to outrun pain anymore. I'm here to meet it. To sit with it. To heal it.

So, I rest. I breathe. I keep going.

And when I forget who I am, I ask for a sign. I hope you do too.

Part Four

LIVING UNMASKED

Chapter 17

WHERE I AM NOW

I'm not fixed—because I was never broken.

I'm not healed in the past-tense, tied-up-with-a-bow kind of way. But I *am* living. Freely. Fully. As *me*.

Today, I no longer confuse productivity with worth. I no longer build my life around people-pleasing or perfection. I no longer feel the need to explain, shrink, or apologize for my sensitivity, my structure, or my need for stillness. I honor my capacity. I trust my nervous system. And most of all—I trust *myself*.

I've built a life that makes room for my truth. My relationships are fewer, but deeper. My work is richer, because I show up as my whole self—not just the polished version. I no longer crave constant motion. I crave peace. And for the first time, I know how to *feel it*.

I still have hard days. I still get dysregulated, overwhelmed, and uncertain. But I don't abandon myself when that happens anymore. I meet myself with curiosity, not criticism. That's the real shift.

I live with intention now. Not to control everything—but to stay connected to what matters.

And that's what healing gave me: Not a new personality. But a home within myself.

Lessons: Stages Of Trauma Recovery
Relearning Safety, Rewriting the Story, Reclaiming the Self

Healing isn't a clean line or a neat timeline; it's a winding, jagged, often brutal process that loops back on itself. We don't "recover" in the sense of going back to who we were. We evolve—through layers of grief, truth, and rebuilding. We grow, scared and wiser, into someone new.

This chapter reframes trauma recovery not as a singular

transformation, but as an ongoing evolution. One where knowing yourself—your nervous system, your trauma responses, your patterns—isn't just useful ... it's necessary.

Stage One: Safety and Stabilization
Learning to breathe when your whole body is bracing for impact

Before healing can begin, safety must be established—not just physically, but in emotional, psychological, and relational aspects. That may mean stepping back from chaos, identifying safe spaces, or finally honoring the part of you that says, "I can't do this alone anymore."

- **Create Internal and External Safety**: Emotional safety might mean setting boundaries with toxic people, building consistency into your day, or slowly reconnecting to your own body.

- **Build Support Systems**: Whether through therapy, community, or a few trusted people—support matters. Healing was never meant to be done in isolation.

Reality Check: If you grew up in dysfunction, stability might feel unfamiliar or even boring. But stability is the nervous system's way of recalibrating. It's not a failure of your trauma response; it's a reset.

Stage Two: Acknowledgment and Acceptance
Facing the reality you've avoided, minimized, or rewritten

This is where the work deepens. The stories you've buried start surfacing. The truth becomes harder to ignore. You stop gaslighting yourself into thinking "it wasn't that bad."

- **Name the Pain**: Whether it was abuse, neglect, loss, or chaos—call it what it was. Not to dwell, but to disarm it.

- **Validate the Emotions**: Rage, sorrow, numbness, shame—none of them are wrong. They are all the data points in your healing map.

Reality Check: You'll be tempted to bypass this part. You'll intellectualize, distract, deny. But unresolved pain doesn't disappear; it just shapeshifts. Processing it starts here. In order to heal, you must feel.

Stage Three: Processing the Trauma
When the real work begins—body, mind, and spirit

Processing is where the trauma gets metabolized. It's also where most people feel like quitting—because this is where things start surfacing.

- **Trauma Therapy**: EMDR, cognitive behavioral therapy (CBT), DBT, somatic work—these are tools, not fixes. They help the brain and body reconnect after trauma's disconnection.

- **Narrative Reconstruction**: Telling your story in a way that's true to you—not sanitized for others. Journaling. Talking. Crying. Naming. Owning.

Reality Check: Processing doesn't mean forgetting or no longer hurting. It means learning how to carry your story without it controlling you.

Stage Four: Grieving and Mourning
Releasing what trauma took—and who you used to be

Trauma steals. From innocence to identity, it leaves behind gaps where there once was wholeness. This stage is about grieving the pieces you lost.

- **Mourn What Was Taken**: Relationships that didn't survive, parts of yourself that dimmed, safety that was never offered—this all deserves to be grieved.

- **Practice Self-Compassion**: Offer yourself the tenderness you were once denied. You are not weak for grieving; you are wise.

Reality Check: Grief doesn't follow a calendar. It resurfaces with anniversaries, smells, songs, dreams. Let it. You don't need to be "over it" to move through it.

Stage Five: Reconnection and Integration
Rebuilding who you are—without the mask, without the old scripts

Now comes the reclamation. Not a return to your "old self"—but the unveiling of your truest one.

- **Relearn Connection**: You begin building relationships that aren't rooted in survival or appeasement. You learn to trust again—not blindly, but bravely.

- **Integrate the New Self**: The trauma is a chapter, not the whole story. You get to decide who you are now—and who you're becoming.

Reality Check: It's okay to miss the old version of you. Even the dysfunctional parts served a purpose. But your healing isn't abandonment—it's integration.

Stage Six: Meaning-Making and Growth
Turning wounds into wisdom—without romanticizing the pain

This stage isn't about glorifying trauma. It's about making sense of it. About choosing to transform what broke you into something honest, useful, or even sacred.

- **Find the Meaning**: This could look like advocacy, writing, helping others, or simply living more fully.

- **Grow From the Rubble**: Not because the trauma "made you stronger"—but because you chose to grow anyway.

Reality Check: You don't have to turn your pain into a career or a cause. Sometimes, surviving and living with intention is the most radical act of all.

What I've Learned Along the Way

- **Unconditional love does not mean unconditional tolerance**. Boundaries are love. For yourself, first.

- **Healing is messy and nonlinear**. There is no before-and-after—only deeper versions of you.

- **This system is not built for your wholeness**. So, the act of healing, resting, and reconnecting to your truth? That's rebellion.

- **The journey never truly ends**. But every time you loop back, you bring more tools, more insight, more self-trust.

Final Reflections: Keep Swinging

Recovery is not linear. It's a spiral. Each loop brings a new layer to face, a new piece to integrate. And every time you revisit an old wound, you're doing so with a deeper understanding of who you are and what you deserve.

If you're somewhere in the middle—lost, tired, questioning—know this: you're not failing. You're healing. And that's the bravest thing you could ever do.

Keep swinging.

Chapter 18

STILL BECOMING

I'm still healing.

That hasn't changed—and maybe it never will. Because healing isn't a finish line. It's a lifelong practice. A rhythm. A relationship with yourself that deepens over time.

Doing the inner work—the hard, messy, confronting work—has been painful. It meant revisiting every trauma I thought I had already buried. It meant peeling back layers of identity, performance, and survival. It meant facing the parts of myself I once tried to hide.

But it also led me back to her.

The autistic girl in the yellow dress—the one I masked for so long—was still there. Waiting. Not for me to fix her, but to finally *see* her. To comfort her. To walk with her through the world as she is.

And that's what this book has been. Not just a memoir. Not just a guide. But a love letter to that girl. To every part of me I once thought I had to abandon in order to be accepted.

Who knows what *you* will find on your journey?

Maybe it won't be a yellow dress or a diagnosis or a single lightning bolt of clarity. But I can promise you this: You won't regret looking. You won't regret shedding what's false. You won't regret doing the "me-search"—because what you'll uncover is the *authentic you.*

The one that's been waiting for you all along. And the world needs *her.* Not the mask. Not the edited version. But *you.*

Still healing.

Still becoming.

Still worthy—exactly as you are.

The Role of Energy Work in Healing Grief and Trauma

"The power is within you. You can heal your life."
– Louise Hay

Energy work—often viewed as outside the scope of traditional mental health—has been one of the most transformative components of my healing. While some may question its legitimacy, I can't deny the shifts I've felt when tending to the energetic imprints trauma leaves behind. For me, energy work became a sacred bridge: one that connected my grief, my trauma, my spiritual beliefs, and my nervous system. It helped me move from dissociation to groundedness, from burnout to restoration.

Louise Hay was one of the first to introduce me to the belief that healing begins within. She taught that thoughts, energy, and the mind-body connection matter. And in grief—especially after the loss of my brother—her words became a lifeline.

Energy Work as a Complement to Trauma Recovery

Traditional therapy helped me process and name my trauma, but energy work gave my body somewhere to place it. I needed more than insight; I needed release. The kind of release that lives in the body, in the nervous system, and in the silent places grief touches.

One of the first modalities I tried was Reiki. I remember lying still, unsure what to expect. But when the practitioner placed her hands over me, something unlocked. I didn't cry—but it felt like my body did. I left that session feeling lighter, clearer, like part of the grief had finally moved.

Later, I explored past life regression. Regardless of whether you believe in past lives, the process unearthed something sacred. I found patterns—deep fears and emotional loops—that had never made sense in the context of my current life. But through this experience, I found language, release, and a sense of compassion for parts of myself I had previously judged or ignored.

Why Energy Work Matters in Grief and Trauma Healing

Energy work isn't about escaping reality. It's about meeting your experience in its rawest form—and helping it move through your body. Trauma isn't just a psychological experience. It's stored in the nervous system, in our breath, in the tension we carry.

Here's how energy work has helped not only me, but many others—in practical, grounded ways:

1. Releasing Energetic Blockages
Grief stagnates energy. Trauma fragments it. Modalities like Reiki, acupuncture, emotion code healing, and chakra work can bring back flow where there was once stuckness. I once had an emotion code session that left me sobbing—not from sadness, but from release. I didn't know I had been carrying that much until it left.

2. Reconnecting to the Body
Practices like yoga, breathwork, and Qi Gong helped me safely return to my body after trauma had made it feel like a battlefield. These modalities offer a reconnection that is often lost in survival mode.

3. Grounding and Present-Moment Awareness
Grief can make you feel untethered. Energy work offers rituals of return—visualization, grounding meditation, and breath practices that bring you back into your body and the moment you're in. Reiki and breathwork helped anchor me when I felt like I was floating in grief.

4. Facilitating Nervous System Regulation
Energy work works *with* your nervous system, not against it. These modalities invite your body into parasympathetic restoration, which is essential when trauma has kept you in fight, flight, freeze, fawn, or flop.

5. Addressing Healing as a Whole-Person Process
The best energy practitioners I've worked with never claimed to "fix" me. Instead, they reminded me that healing is about align-

ing the mind, body, and spirit. True transformation doesn't just happen on a cognitive level, it happens in the quiet shifts, the subtle energy changes, the moments of stillness and presence.

The Frequency of Authenticity

There's a belief in energy healing that authenticity is one of the highest frequencies we can embody. I've found that to be true. When we drop the mask—when we stop pretending and start feeling—we become energetically aligned with our truest self. Louise Hay's teachings reinforced this for me: When we choose self-love, we align with a power far greater than ourselves.

Through energy work, I learned that healing isn't about controlling what happened to us; it's about releasing how it continues to live inside us. And that release often happens in quiet, sacred spaces that can't always be explained—but are deeply felt.

What Others Have Found

In my work as a therapist, I've seen clients shift in ways that traditional talk therapy alone couldn't offer. One client, after trying Reiki for the first time, described it as "a reset button for my soul." Another said that emotion code healing "unlocked a door I didn't even know I was locked behind." Energy work doesn't replace therapy—it complements it. And sometimes, it accesses places that words can't reach.

A Balanced Healing Approach

Let me be clear: Energy work is not a shortcut or a substitute. It's a tool—one of many—that can support grief and trauma recovery. I still rely on evidence-based therapeutic approaches, community, spirituality, and medication when needed. But energy work gave me a language and practice for parts of my healing that Western models often overlook.

If you're considering energy work, bring curiosity. Bring your discernment. But most of all, bring your intention to heal. These practices aren't magic fixes—they're invitations to go deeper.

Final Reflections: Healing Through the "Juice"

One thing I often tell clients in session is that the process—the muck, the mess, the discomfort—is the "juice." It's the part people look back on and say, "That's when everything changed." We try so hard to skip it. But healing doesn't happen around the juice—it happens in it.

Energy work gave me a way to be in the juice with less fear and more trust. And I still think about that dream I had—the galaxy, the wings, the voice that said, "You know what to do." That dream didn't offer clarity. It offered direction. A direction toward faith, authenticity, and healing. Energy work helped me follow it.

You don't have to believe in energy healing to feel its impact. You just have to be willing to explore what helps you come home to yourself.

The "juice" is the grey area of healing, and you have to feel it to heal it.

Chapter 19

WHAT HELPED: SOLUTIONS THAT MADE HEALING POSSIBLE

There's no one-size-fits-all path to healing. But there are tools, practices, and internal shifts that helped me unmask—not just in theory, but in everyday life.

These weren't quick fixes. They didn't magically make the trauma disappear. But they gave me something even more powerful: Safety. Permission. And choice.

Here's what supported my healing the most—and what might support yours, too:

1. Creating Safety in My Body
Unmasking requires you to feel. But feeling is impossible when your nervous system is stuck in survival.

I started by building tiny pockets of safety—breathwork, grounding, weighted blankets, movement, scent, sound. Regulation became my foundation. Not luxury—necessity.

2. Naming the Mask
I got honest about *when* I was masking—and *why*. Was I people-pleasing? Fawning? Avoiding shame?

I didn't judge myself—I just noticed. Awareness was the first step toward choice.

3. Allowing Discomfort
Healing meant learning how to stay with hard feelings instead of escaping them. I practiced tolerating discomfort in my body, in conversations, in quiet. It wasn't about fixing—it was about *sitting*.

4. Embracing My Neurodivergence
Instead of seeing my autistic traits as flaws, I started honoring them. Structure, routines, sensory accommodations, quiet time—

these became non-negotiables. I stopped performing "normal."
I started living *aligned.*

5. Telling the Truth (Even When it Shakes You)
I began sharing my real story—with myself, with safe people, with
my patients. Truth-telling helped me grieve, connect, and shed the
shame I'd carried. It also gave others permission to do the same.

6. Seeking Help, Spiritually and Clinically
As I went deeper into my own *me-search,* I found myself not just
looking for answers—but for meaning. I started reconnecting with
my spirituality in ways that felt personal, grounding, and sacred.
It wasn't about religion—it was about *remembrance.* A return to
something deeper than logic. I needed something that could hold
not just my mind, but my soul.

And even as a therapist, I knew I couldn't do it alone.

I sought out professionals who could hold the full complexity
of my story—people who wouldn't flinch at my truth, who knew
how to honor both science and spirit. I needed someone to witness *me* the way I witness others. To remind me that my healing
mattered, too. To help me come home to myself, layer by layer.

Because the truth is this: Healing might start with self-awareness, but it *deepens* in relationship—especially the kind built on
trust, safety, and sacred reflection.

7. Reclaiming Joy
Healing isn't just shadow work. It's joy work. I leaned into play,
creativity, music, movement, and moments that made me feel *alive.*
Not because I was "done healing," but because joy is part of healing.

These solutions didn't happen all at once. They unfolded
slowly, over time, with setbacks, resistance, and breakthroughs.
But they taught me that unmasking isn't about becoming someone
new—it's about coming back to who I was *before the world told me
to hide.*

Turning on the Light—Healing Through Quotes and Reflections

> *"Happiness can be found even in the darkest of times,*
> *if one only remembers to turn on the light."*
> – **Albus Dumbledore** (JK Rowling, *Harry Potter and the Prisoner of Azkaban*)

Mantras, quotes, and song lyrics have a unique way of piercing through the fog of trauma and grief. They become anchors—offering clarity, validation, and sometimes just enough light to keep going. In moments when everything else felt overwhelming or hollow, these words became a form of medicine. They were often the first step in reminding me I wasn't alone, that what I was feeling was real, and that healing was still possible.

That Dumbledore quote has followed me for years. I used to think "turning on the light" meant flipping a switch and instantly feeling better. I've learned that's not how it works.

The darkness, especially after trauma or loss, can become deceptively comforting. It feels familiar. Predictable. A place where you don't have to explain, perform, or show up. But over time, it stops protecting you—and starts swallowing you. The silence grows louder. The numbness gets heavier. And eventually, you hit a moment where you either sink deeper—or decide to fight your way out.

That's what "turning on the light" became for me: a conscious decision to stop waiting for someone else to rescue me and start showing up for myself.

Quotes That Helped Me Heal

Here are some of the words that illuminated my own healing process—each one a flashlight in a moment of darkness:

> *"Trauma comes back as a reaction, not a memory."*
> **—Bessel van der Kolk**

"We don't heal in isolation; we heal in community."
—Suki Baxter

"Unexpressed emotions will never die. They are buried alive
and will come forth later in uglier ways."
—Sigmund Freud

"Trauma is what happens inside you, not what happens to you."
—Gabor Maté

"If you are going through hell, keep going."
—Winston Churchill

These words didn't fix my pain, but they named it. They reminded me that healing is a path others have walked—and that it's okay to take that path slowly, one quote, one moment, at a time.

Reflections on the Healing Journey

The quotes above aren't just wise sayings. They speak to core truths about the messy, nonlinear process of healing. Here's what they've taught me:

1. Acknowledging the Darkness

The first step in healing is recognizing that you're in it. Denial often masquerades as control, but it only delays the reckoning. As Bessel van der Kolk wrote, trauma doesn't always return as a clear memory—it often resurfaces in your reactions, behaviors, or chronic patterns. Naming that experience is the beginning of unlearning it.

2. Finding the Light

Turning on the light doesn't mean everything is okay. It means you're willing to look. To reach for the parts of you that still believe in joy, in peace, in something beyond the pain. Light can come through laughter, music, movement, touch, or even a quote that meets you where you are.

3. The Power of Community

Healing doesn't happen in a vacuum. As Suki Baxter reminds us, we heal in community. Whether it's a friend, therapist, support group, or spiritual connection, being seen and heard by others accelerates the healing process. Pain isolates—connection repairs.

4. Expressing the Unspoken

Unexpressed emotions don't disappear. They bury themselves in our bodies, our relationships, our habits. Expressing them—through writing, crying, talking, or creative outlets—helps us release what we've been holding onto. We don't just talk to heal; we express to integrate.

5. Continuing Anyway

There were days I wanted to give up. Days I thought I had regressed or failed. But Churchill's quote echoed in my mind: "If you're going through hell, keep going." Because stopping only lets the fire consume you. Walking forward—however slowly—is its own form of defiance and healing.

Quotes as Tools for Trauma Recovery

Quotes have served as both mirrors and compasses—reflecting where I am and pointing me toward where I want to go. They've reframed shame, softened inner criticism, and reminded me of the universal truths buried beneath personal pain.

When you find one that resonates, don't just read it—anchor it. Tape it in your bathroom mirror. Save it to your phone. Scribble it in the margins of your journal. Let it be a reminder of who you are when you forget.

Create Your Own Healing Roadmap

I invite you to start your own collection of mantras, quotes, or song lyrics that speak to your soul. Make them part of your healing ritual. Let them guide you when you feel lost or disconnected.

What we feed our mind matters—especially when the mind has been shaped by trauma. These words aren't a substitute for healing work, but they can be a catalyst. A reminder that healing is possible. That the darkness isn't permanent. That the light is still there, waiting for you to reach for it.

Final Reflections: Be Your Own Light

I've come to learn that healing isn't about erasing the darkness; it's about learning how to carry the light. Sometimes that light is a quote. Sometimes it's a voice in your head telling you to keep going. And sometimes, it's the quiet knowing that you've survived before and you will again.

You don't need to be fully healed to be worthy. You don't need to have it all figured out to keep moving. You just need to remember:

You can turn on the light. And when you do—it changes everything.

Chapter 20

DIFFERENT WOUNDS, DIFFERENT HEALING

If there's one thing I've learned on this journey, it's this: Healing is not one-size-fits-all.

We often speak about "trauma" as a singular category, but the truth is, each trauma I've experienced required a different part of me to heal.

Some wounds needed silence. Others needed to be screamed out loud. Some asked for stillness. Others demanded movement, fire, tears, sweat, and voice.

The *early traumas*—the isolation, the abandonment, the sexual assault—shaped my nervous system. They taught me to mask, to over-function, to anticipate rejection before it arrived. Healing those wounds meant going deep into the roots. It required inner child work. It meant re-parenting myself, unlearning shame, and giving voice to the parts of me that were never allowed to speak.

It meant learning that safety *had to exist inside me* before I could ever trust it outside of me.

The *later traumas*—the loss of my brother, the numbing, the spiraling and chaos—tore through the version of me I had built to survive. Healing those traumas felt more like rebuilding from rubble.

It meant confronting guilt. Sitting in the silence of grief. Learning to live with the ache of unanswerable questions. It wasn't about "fixing" anything—it was about *staying*. Staying with the pain. Staying with the memory. Staying with myself, even when it hurt.

It also meant choosing life again and again—not out of obligation, but out of reverence. For him. For me. For the people still here.

Yes, there were common threads in the healing: Self-compassion. Nervous system regulation. Professional support. Spiritual seeking. But each trauma had its own texture. Its own voice. Its own timeline.

And each one required a different version of me to show up. Not a *better* version—just a more present one.

Some days, healing looked like setting boundaries. Other days, it looked like lying on the floor and letting myself cry. Some parts of me needed strength. Others needed softness. And all of it was valid.

That's the truth I want you to walk away with:

Your healing won't look like mine. Your trauma won't respond to one neat prescription. And that's okay.

There's no wrong way to heal—only the way that feels most honest to *you*.

Conclusion

Owning the Story, Reclaiming the Self

Writing this book began as an exploration of trauma. It became something else entirely—something I hadn't expected: a mirror, a reckoning, and a return. It turned into a process of remembering the parts of myself I had long buried beneath achievement, perfectionism, and survival. It was never just about writing a book. It was about coming home to myself.

From the very beginning, I knew healing wouldn't be linear. I've said it throughout these pages, and I will say it again now: The journey isn't a straight line—it loops, spirals, and pulls us back to places we thought we had long since outgrown. What I didn't anticipate was how many old wounds still needed tending, how many stories I had been carrying that weren't mine, and how deeply I had been living in a performance of protection rather than in a truth of presence.

This process forced me to slow down. To confront the trauma drive beneath my ambition. To acknowledge the exhaustion that came from years of masking and adapting. To unearth the grief I had numbed. To finally meet the neurodivergent identity I had always felt but never fully seen. These layers weren't just chapters in this book—they were the blueprint of my becoming.

I have spent most of my life surviving. This book is my decision to live.

A Testament and an Offering

This book is my story, but it is also an offering.
To the ones who've felt invisible.
To those who have questioned their worth.
To anyone who has been told they are too much, too emotional, too loud, too intense.
To the ones still trying to find their voice.
To the ones still afraid to use it.

May these words remind you that your story is valid. That your pain is not too heavy. That your healing matters—not because it's perfect or finished, but because it's *yours*.

If this book gives you anything, let it be this:

Permission.

To feel.

To question.

To rage.

To rest.

To be.

To take up space without apology.

Embracing the Unfinished Journey

Healing is not a destination. It is not a checklist. It is not a milestone we reach and never look back. It is a living, breathing relationship we have with ourselves—a commitment to keep going, to keep unlearning, and to keep choosing truth over comfort.

I no longer want to be the version of me that existed before trauma. That version is gone—and I do not mourn her. I honor who I have become because of what I've endured. I no longer see my intensity, my sensitivity, or my hunger for justice as flaws. They are my gifts. My compass. My fuel.

For so long, I feared that unmasking would leave me exposed, raw, and unsafe. But the truth is this: the mask never protected me. It only distanced me—from others, from joy, from myself. Taking it off didn't break me. It freed me.

To Those Still in the Process

If you're still deep in it—still unraveling, still questioning, still trying to find the ground under your feet—I see you. I know how heavy it can feel. I know the weariness that comes from performing, from hiding, from bending yourself into versions you were never meant to be.

Please hear this:

You are not alone.

You are not broken.

And you do not need to become anyone else to be worthy of love or rest or joy.

You are not behind. You are becoming.

Let this book be a companion on the days when it's too hard to say out loud what you're feeling. Let these pages be proof that transformation is possible—even if it's slow. Especially if it's slow.

A Final Reflection

I thought I was writing a book about trauma. But what I wrote—what I uncovered—was a book about self-acceptance. About remembering who I was before the world told me who I needed to be. About reclaiming the girl in the yellow dress. About honoring the fire I had buried beneath performance and perfectionism.

This is not the end of the story. It's the beginning of a new chapter—not just for me, but for anyone who's ready to live without apology.

So, if you're reading this and wondering if it's time to unmask, if it's time to speak, if it's time to come home to yourself—consider this your invitation.

You don't need permission. But just in case you do, here it is. I'll meet you on the other side.

With love and resilience,
Kaitlyn Elizabeth Kenealy, MA, LPC
Your autistic author and therapist

Acknowledgements

To those who have walked beside me on this journey—thank you.

To my family and friends who have supported me through the highs and lows, your unwavering belief in me has made this possible.

To my patients, colleagues, and fellow mental health advocates—you inspire me daily with your courage and vulnerability. Thank you for trusting me, for letting me walk with you in your healing, and for reminding me of the strength in being seen.

To the neurodivergent community, thank you for reminding me that our voices matter, our experiences are valid, and that unmasking is both a personal and collective revolution.

To my incredible team—editors, publishers, and everyone who helped bring this book to life—your dedication and hard work mean the world to me.

And finally, to the readers who pick up this book, whether out of curiosity, solidarity, or a deep longing for understanding—I see you, I honor you, and I hope this book helps you see yourself more clearly.

I know in my first book I told you: I hope you step into the arena and swing.

In this book, I hope to remind you that you deserve to take up space. You matter. You are worthy of being seen, heard, and celebrated—exactly as you are.

About the Author

Kaitlyn Elizabeth Kenealy, MA, LPC, is an award-winning psychotherapist, bestselling author, speaker, and CEO of *Into the Woods Wellness*—a multidisciplinary healing space dedicated to uncovering the root causes of pain and guiding individuals toward lasting, integrative wellness.

Holding master's degrees in both Community and Mental Health Counseling and Gender and Women's Studies, Kaitlyn blends clinical expertise with lived experience to offer a radically honest and compassionate approach to healing.

Her debut book, *Healing is Messy AF,* resonated with readers around the world for its unfiltered truth and emotional depth. In her follow-up, *Unmasking: A Journey Through Trauma, Truth, and a Spectrum of Healing,* she deepens the conversation—guiding readers through the complexities of trauma, identity, neurodivergence, and the long arc of becoming.

Beyond her work, Kaitlyn finds joy in music, art, and spending intentional time with her husband, family, and especially her nieces and nephews—a role she treasures deeply. She lives in Wisconsin with her fiercely loyal cat, Loki, and continues to lead, write, and heal from a place of purpose, integrity, and heart.

She believes healing is not a destination, but a spectrum of becoming.

Notes

Notes

Notes

www.ingramcontent.com/pod-product-compliance
Lightning Source LLC
Chambersburg PA
CBHW031050160726
47991CB00005B/2091